MW00606018

Divorce Resiliency

Release the Trauma of Your Divorce and Reconnect with Your Best Self

Sherry L. Smith, LMFT, CDC®

Copyright © 2020 Sherry L. Smith LMFT, CDC®

ISBN: 978-1-7350655-0-2

All rights reserved.

No part of this publication may be reproduced, stored in a retrieval system, or transmitted, in any form or by other means, electronic, mechanical, photocopying, recording, or otherwise, without prior written permission of the author.

The fact that an individual, organization, or website is referred to in this work as a citation and/or potential source of further information does not mean that the author endorses the information the individual, organization, or website may provide or recommendations they/it may make. Further, readers should be aware that websites listed in this work may have changed or disappeared between when this work was written and when it's read.

"Where you stumble, there lies your treasure"... Joseph Campbell

Dedication

This book is dedicated to Elizabeth Banks and Susan Gertzman. We went through our divorces together and supported each other through our own 6-Month Thaw period. Also, to my dear friends and Goddesses Extraordinaire Karen Littlefield, Tamra Daws, Debbi Walker, Anne Crabtree, Rowan Griffiths, Lorelei Lindow, Stephanie Read and my sister Joan Vanbuuren. This amazing tribe of women have accompanied me on my own divorce journey at various times. It has been said that the people you surround yourself with are the mirror to your soul. Thanks to the light each of you shine into my life, my soul is dazzling!

I would also like to dedicate this book to my Aunt, Ruth Hill, who always provided a safe place for me to land, as well as my brother, Brad Smith, who has been a source of unbending support. In addition, to my parents, Joe and Peggy Smith, who, I hope, are smiling down on me from heaven. Not only did they give me life, but they have also been my greatest teachers.

Finally, I dedicate this book to the countless women who have had the courage to be vulnerable and trusted me enough to accompany them as they reconnected with the best version of themselves. These women are a constant source of inspiration for me!

Table of Contents

Preface

In order to protect the privacy of my clients, I have used fictional characters in this book. These characters were inspired by the countless clients who have trusted me enough to allow me to accompany them on their divorce journey. With these clients, I have noticed some common themes. These themes were used to craft the case studies included in this book.

In my practice, I mostly work with heterosexual females and a few heterosexual males. I do have some clients from the LGBTQ community and thoroughly enjoy working with them, but based on the demographics of where my practice is located, I don't have the opportunity to work with them often. Having said this, the examples used here are provided through a heterosexual lens. I have found relationship dynamics to be universal no matter a person's sexual or gender orientation, so the information shared here is appropriate for anyone.

Please note that although I work with people who are dealing with divorce, I am not an attorney. Information provided in this book comes from my experience with my clients, my training and life experience. It is not to be considered legal advice. Legal questions tend to be specific to the area where you live so it is in your best interest to consult with an attorney licensed in your state or province.

If you are having suicidal thoughts, please contact the suicide hotline at 800-273-8255, call 911 or go to your nearest emergency room. If you feel you or your children are in danger, please contact local law enforcement immediately or the Domestic Violence Hotline 800-799-7233.

Chapter 1

So this is it…I'm getting a divorce

Imagine yourself as a little girl. You're playing with your Barbies and setting up a wedding scene. As you set up the scene, you create your own ideal wedding scene in your mind. You imagine yourself in your gorgeous white flowing wedding dress, make-up perfectly applied and hair flawlessly swept up to set off the sparkly earrings adorning your ears. As you start the long walk down the aisle, all eyes are on you. Not a dry eye in the place. Your beloved stands at the end of your journey, tears flowing down his cheeks as he gazes upon your loveliness. That little girl never imagined anything other than a lifetime of love, joy and peace with her Prince Charming. So here you are now, reading this book and facing the terrifying unknown, life as a divorced woman. This is not likely the outcome you planned for yourself when you were growing up. You imagined your life with a devoted husband. Maybe you imagined having children together. Now, if you have children, you are most likely consumed with thoughts of their care and how the divorce will affect them. You also wonder if you are emotionally equipped to care for them in the way they need you to right now. Please know that you are not alone in your pain.

Divorce is one of life's greatest tragedies. In those painful tragedies that we don't see coming, we are presented with the opportunity for the greatest personal growth. So wipe your tears and congratulate yourself for taking the first step towards becoming a more self-aware and evolved version of yourself. The new you will be wiser, more balanced and enjoy an inner peace, joy and happiness beyond anything you can imagine from where you sit right now.

Who am I and How Can I Help You?

I am a Licensed Marriage and Family Therapist, a Certified Divorce Coach®, a child of divorce and a divorced woman. In my practice, I specialize in working with women who are going through the same experience as you are right now. My intention with this book is not only to prepare you for what's to come but, more importantly, to arm you with the tools needed to release the trauma of divorce and reconnect with the highest version of yourself.

I am often asked why I choose to do this work. That is, work with people who are dealing with one of life's most difficult transitions. For me, it's a calling of sorts. I feel my life was set-up from the time I was a child to do this work. My clients come to me as they are about to enter the birth canal. After a period of pain, they will be reborn. I view myself as the midwife there to help them through that process.

My parents went through a high-conflict divorce after 29-years of marriage that started when they separated the day before my senior year of high school. My sister and I had just gone to see the first "Rocky" movie, a matinee. It was a warm, sunny Sunday in August and we came home to find my mother with a packed suitcase, calmly explaining to us that she had had enough and was moving in with our Aunt Ruth. My father was not in the house when she told us. I don't know if she asked him to leave or what happened while we were at the movie...it is a mystery to me but it was a surreal moment that seemed eerily peaceful given the circumstances. Looking back on it, I see it as the calm before the storm, so to speak. I can't speak for my sister but it caught me off-guard because they seemed to have worked through their issues and were in a happier place.

My parent's marriage was never an easy one. My father, who was generally a funny, charming man with a sharp mind, varied interests, and a photographic memory that enabled him to have vast knowledge on a variety of topics, had previously been an abusive alcoholic. He was eventually able to maintain a long recovery in a 12-step program but still had some abusive tendencies that were rooted in childhood trauma that he never addressed. Early in their marriage, when I was about 6-years old and he was still drinking, I remember outbursts of physical abuse and the police being called. Mom would take my brother, sister and me to my Aunt Ruth's house when that happened, who would provide a fun environment for us to help distract us from what had happened at home.

My mother, a former beauty queen who had married at 19-years old and had no education beyond a high school diploma, had some health problems that prevented her from staying employed. She also had some unhealthy codependent patterns rooted in her own childhood. Having said this, she was an incredibly strong woman who was finally able to overcome the health issues with a life-changing surgery. She was then able to start a career while finishing her education. She worked her way up from the typing pool of an insurance company to a regional marketing position where she managed a territory of independent insurance agents. I have tremendous admiration for her and consider her one of my biggest role models. As an adult, I now understand the sacrifices she made to keep her family together, but I also recognize the consequences of being raised in a toxic, dysfunctional environment. I often question why she stayed in the marriage but also realize the choices she made were largely informed by her generational attitudes about family.

My parents had separated and reconciled a few times over the years and seemed to go in cycles of happiness and misery. Despite their dysfunctional cycle, they loved each other deeply. Because of this cycle of separation and reconciliation, when Mom told us she was leaving that day, I didn't quite believe it would be permanent this time. I was proven wrong. This time around, it was permanent, and our family was ripped apart in the process.

At the time of the split, I was 17-years old. I love my Mom and Dad, who are now both deceased, but they did everything wrong in their divorce, and I mean EVERYTHING! I'm sure that comes as no surprise when I describe their relationship dynamic. Not only did they put me in the middle of their arguments, but my mother would speak negatively about my father to me. My father, who I was living with at the time because my mother had moved out, went off the deep-end emotionally and was in a constant state of rage. It quickly became apparent how much our mother buffered us from his anger. He took out a lot of his anger on me, threatening at one point to throw my things out in the front yard and change the locks. You can imagine how mortified a 17-year old would have been if this had happened. I don't even recall what prompted his anger in this particular case, in fact, much of this time in my life I have blocked out of my memory. It felt as though my teenage world was turned upside down. I do recall, partying more than usual and my grades slipping (I was typically a very good student). Through a therapeutic lens, I now see this behavior as a call for help. I didn't tell any of my friends or teachers my entire senior year what my life at home had become. I presented as if everything was perfectly normal. My parents were so obsessed with their anger at each other and I somehow got lost in it all.

I eventually moved in with my mother and my Aunt Ruth where we lived until Mom was able to buy her own place. I lived in three places in the course of my senior year of high school and no one outside of my family knew a thing. I stuffed all my fear, anxiety and sadness. In the course of all of this, no one even considered or discussed getting me help by putting me into therapy.

I was the youngest of three children. My 21-year old sister, who was also living at home, took on the role of my father's confidant in an effort to keep him calm and emotionally regulated, a lot of responsibility for someone her age. My brother, at 23-years old, was not living at home during this time and, thankfully, was able to buffer himself from the drama happening there. In my parent's defense, this occurred in the 1980's when there weren't the resources there are now.

The trauma from their divorce followed me to college as my

college tuition was a point of contention for them during the divorce settlement. Needless to say, the partying that started my senior year of high school got worse and I eventually dropped out of college and moved to Atlanta to be with my first love who just happened to also be a drug dealer. The first sign of how the divorce was impacting my choices and how I showed up in relationships.

That trauma stayed with me into adulthood, impacting my marriage, which ultimately also ended in divorce, until I finally found healing. I put myself back into college, while working full-time, finishing my bachelor degree, then, later in life, a master's degree in Marriage and Family Therapy at 45-years old, eventually becoming a Certified Divorce Coach®. My mission is to use my training in family systems and divorce coaching combined with years of research and life experience to help others do divorce in a way that minimizes trauma to the family system. A big part of this mission is to help women who have lost themselves in their marriage or while raising children reconnect with the best version of themselves. Once they have reconnected with themselves, they are better able to co-parent and show up for their kids.

I view my life as "before therapist" and "after therapist." I believe it took me learning about relationship dynamics and how to communicate in a healthier way in my master's program, then applying that knowledge to help my clients, to finally release my own negative relationship patterns rooted in childhood dysfunction. With this book, I am passing this knowledge on to you. Not only did I survive, and eventually thrive, beyond my childhood divorce experience, but I used this experience to gain knowledge to help you and your family do the same. Believe it or not, it is possible for you, and more importantly, your children to flourish after divorce.

Chapter 2

Marriage, Divorce and Our Society

In our society, we place a high value on marriage. Although divorce rates have been declining based on the latest Census Bureau Statistics (2000-2017), they still hover around 45%. For marriages 20 years or longer, the rate is around 52%. For subsequent marriages, the rate is even higher. These numbers are controversial, because they are based on people who are married and don't take into account that more people are choosing not to marry these days. Having said this, I'm sure we can all agree these rates are still pretty high. However, more money is being spent on weddings than ever. According to a popular wedding planning site called "The Knot" (Seaver 2019), a survey of 30,000 couples who married in 2018 indicated the average cost of a wedding was $33,931. That's down slightly from $35,329 in 2016 and up from $28,427 in 2012 (these numbers don't include honeymoon spending). One only has to take a quick look at Pinterest to see how much space is devoted to wedding planning. Considering this data, it's easy to imagine why divorce is so difficult. Not only because of the dominant narrative in our society that people should be married to be happy, but also based on how much we apparently include being "married" as our identity. The influence of social media and a newsfeed full of everyone's "highlight reel" have only reinforced the dominant narrative.

When a decision to divorce has been made, whether you made the decision or your spouse did, it can feel as though your identity is being taken away. You immediately start to question who you are and what you know to be reality. Perhaps you feel you have lost control of your circumstances and as if the rug was pulled out from under you. It can feel traumatic and all-consuming. Not only are you feeling overwhelmed, but you likely feel very alone in your experience. I work mostly with women and have had more than one client tell me that when they are going through divorce and are out in public, they are very aware of which women are wearing wedding rings. They state that they feel inadequate in comparison, when they know nothing about these married women and their circumstances! It doesn't help when others project their opinions about marriage onto us. My manicurist recently said in passing while doing my nails "there is something wrong with you if you aren't married." I think she must have forgotten what I do for a living. I later found out she is unhappy in her marriage and involved in an emotional affair.

Sometimes it is helpful to put things in perspective by taking the emotion out of it for a moment and looking at it statistically. According to Our World Data (Roser, 2019) our life expectancy has increased over the years. In fact, as Roser states, before the 19th century life expectancy averaged somewhere around 30-40 years old. Since 1900, global life expectancy has more than doubled to above 70 years old.

As indicated in an article titled "How Long Do Average Marriages Last?" from the website The Balance (Lake, 2019) the average length of a marriage in the United States is approximately 7 years. I find in my practice based in a middle to upper class suburban area of Charlotte, NC "till death do us part" is around 20-25 years. While that may have been a lifelong marriage 100 years ago when people weren't living as long, now as people live longer, they often outgrow each other in this length of time. When looking at marriage through this lens, it appears we are moving in the direction where divorce and multiple marriages are more common.

Some view marriage itself as remnants of a patriarchal society and are choosing alternative methods to do relationships more consciously outside the confines of marriage. Having said all of this, my goal here is not to suggest that marriages can't be happy. Marriage can be richly rewarding, deep and fulfilling if both of you love each other and are willing to do the work. I see it on a regular basis in my office. We are, afterall, wired for connection. In many cases, when a client comes to me experiencing marriage ambiguity, we are able to determine that there is still hope in the marriage and the client works to successfully repair the marriage with her husband. Having said this, the research shows that couple's wait on average 6-years too late to get help. If you are experiencing the trauma of divorce, recognizing that you are experiencing trauma can help with the healing process.

Chapter 3

Is Divorce Really Trauma?

In the therapeutic community, we view trauma as big "T" trauma or little "t" trauma. Big "T" trauma usually meets the DSM-V criteria for PTSD and involves events such as living through a combat situation in the military, surviving a life threatening event or surviving rape, incest, sexual or physical abuse. Little "t" trauma is usually caused by divorce, relationship conflict, grief and loss, financial hardship, etc. It can be extremely distressing for a person but may not meet the criteria for PTSD. It's important to make this distinction because some people going through a divorce associate trauma with PTSD and feel what they are experiencing somehow doesn't compare. I find the trauma associated with divorce is highly individualized, can be extremely painful and is not to be minimized. Having said this, if you are are having suicidal thoughts or urges, please call the suicide hotline immediately 800-273-8255, call 911 or go to your nearest emergency room.

Finding meaning in the trauma

In my own experience, as well as what I have observed to be the experience of my clients who thrive post-divorce, it's crucial to be able to find meaning from your divorce experience. In order to do that, it is helpful to take a look at the relationship from a systemic perspective and try to understand your role in it's demise and any dysfunction that you can own. This is the first step in getting realigned with your higher self. This process may be easier to do once you have had some time to process your grief. Time and distance tend to help you gain perspective, so you may need to revisit this section later.

I'd like to start by giving an abridged version of the Bowby's Attachment Theory (David, 2016) and how it plays out in marriages. Bowby states from his research that our experience in childhood with our primary caregivers in terms of what was modeled for us, as well as any attachment injuries that might have occurred in childhood, can have a big impact on our relationships as an adult. There are two main attachment styles, secure and insecure. The book "Attached" by Amir Levine and Rachel Heller is an excellent resource if you'd like to educate yourself further on this theory. The book also includes an assessment where you can determine your own attachment style.

Under the "secure" heading, in the family of origin Mom and Dad were present and physically and emotionally available for their children. They showed-up and followed-through when they were supposed to and did what they said they were going to do. Parents modeled for their children how to do healthy conflict and repair after conflict. The home was loving and filled with good structure and routine. If the child was going through any stress or emotional turmoil, the parents were there for them in an appropriate way with healthy boundaries. These kids were free to be kids. Folks lucky enough to have this type of childhood tend to grow up and have happy, successful marriages and lives.

With an insecure attachment style, the child does not benefit from the same stable environment. In the childhood home there might have existed physical, emotional or sexual abuse. Perhaps there was substance abuse or alcoholism. Likely there was physical or emotional unavailability of one or both parents. Maybe there was an overly anxious or enmeshed parent such as a "helicopter" parent who exhibited extreme anxiety in parenting. The boundaries were not clear for these children so they felt anxiety, tension and stress as a child. In some cases, children became "parentified" in these situations and had to take on adult responsibility to make sure they and their siblings are cared for appropriately. Sometimes, one of the parents did not get their needs met from their spouse, so they turned towards one or more of their children to fulfill their emotional needs, which can feel overwhelming for a child. There are a host of other examples not listed here but I think you get the idea. In these scenarios, the child is not free to be a child and, somewhere along the way, internalized the message that it's not safe to be vulnerable. Perhaps they learned that they aren't allowed to have a voice or opinion because they learned that when they expressed themselves, there are negative repercussions. These children tend to grow up to have either anxious, avoidant or disorganized/disoriented attachment styles.

For the purposes of this demonstration, I'm going to work with the first two insecure styles, anxious and avoidant. In romantic relationships, the anxious style and avoidant style attract to each other like a magnet. I have found in my practice working with couples that one will lean one way and one will lean the other. Once these two are in a relationship, an anxious/avoidant dance will ensue with the anxious partner being the one to pursue in times of stress and the avoidant partner being the one to distance.

In order to illustrate this dance, I'm going to give a fictitious example. I will acknowledge that this example includes gender biases but this is a typical scenario of insecure attachment styles playing out. Keep in mind, the example is less about the "content" of the argument. There is something deeper going on that I'll explain at the end.

Let's say Mom, we'll call her Diane, is the anxious partner and she is responsible for cooking dinner and cleaning up after dinner. She stays home with the couple's small children and is in charge of running the household. She is exhausted and stretched thin emotionally from her 24-hour a day job. She has lost her identity in being a mother and wife and feels angry often. She has no time for self-care. Dad, we'll refer to him as Bob, who is the financial provider with a long commute to and from work, is responsible for taking out the trash after dinner. This was something Bob begrudgingly agreed to at some point even though in the back of his mind he knew he wasn't going to follow-through because he doesn't feel appreciated in the relationship. He just didn't want to have a fight with Diane in the moment when this topic was discussed, so he just agreed to it to appease her.

Well, every night after dinner Bob goes immediately to the couch and starts getting engrossed in his phone. Diane has to ask Bob 2 or 3 times to take out the trash. Over time, Diane starts to resent this and one night explodes "you NEVER (insert swear word) take out the trash! I have to ask 100 times every night!!!" Bob, who feels attacked because it seems as though this is coming from out of the blue, immediately gets defensive "I work all day to provide for this family! Not to mention the fact that I have an hour commute each way! I deserve to sit on the couch and unwind! I'll take out the trash when I'm damn good and ready! All you do is nag me! I can't do anything right! All I am is a paycheck around here!"

Diane, who is now furious, takes it to a new level. She gets in his face pointing at him and sneering "you never respect me! It's like I'm invisible to you! I might as well be your maid!" Bob, throws up his hands and stomps out of the room (distances) and slams the door to the bedroom. Diane, appalled that Bob has had the audacity to walk away from her in the middle of an argument, goes after him (pursues). At this point the argument escalates to new proportions with each party screaming and swearing at each other until Diane walks away in tears. For a period of time they stay away from each other, the tension is palpable, until they calm down and Bob comes back around and starts being nice because he doesn't like the tension. Diane, who doesn't want to fight anymore and just wants to feel emotionally connected to her husband, starts being nice back and the original conflict topic never gets brought back up until the next fight when it all comes back out, along with all the other unresolved issues they have argued over.

Perhaps this scenario is making you cringe a little because some version of it sounds familiar. Maybe arguments between you and your spouse never escalated to this level but the dance was similar. As I mentioned, the content of the argument, the trash, is not what this is about. It's about a fear of vulnerability. Not feeling safe to express your true emotions. In this case, Diane was feeling disrespected and ignored. Perhaps some childhood abandonment issues were being triggered when Bob checked out of the relationship with his phone. If she could have learned how to communicate from this vulnerable place in a productive way while she was in a calmer state, and assuming Bob knew how to create a safe place and sit with his negative feelings in order to allow her to express herself, this conversation might have gone a whole different way.

I'm a big fan of Brene Brown who has done a tremendous amount of research on vulnerability. If you aren't familiar with her work and would like to learn more, you should start with her YouTube video, The Power of Vulnerability (2010). I suggest it to most of my clients as an entree into the importance of vulnerability in relationships.

In our society, we tend to view vulnerability as a weakness, when it is actually a strength. It takes courage and risk to put oneself out there in a vulnerable way and hope it lands in a safe place. It also takes accountability to own and communicate our vulnerability, not knowing the outcome of doing so, without blaming others or self-medicating our negative feelings. When we are raised in an insecure environment, we learn unhealthy defense mechanisms to protect ourselves from feeling vulnerable. In order to do relationships in a healthier way, we need to learn healthier ways of communicating. It helps to release the shame around your learned negative relationship patterns. Afterall, we can't pick our parents! But as an adult, we can make a different choice.

Dr. Susan Johnson, the founder of Emotionally Focused Therapy for couples, has done amazing work on how attachment styles play out in relationships and helps couples learn to identify and communicate their primary emotions. Dr. John Gottman, the founder of The Gottman Method, has years of data based on his research on how couples interact as well and is able to predict divorce with 93.6% accuracy when observing couples communicate. He provides methods of how to identify negative communication patterns and communicate in a healthier way.

Identifying your own attachment style is the first step to not only recognizing your role in the breakdown of your marriage, but also to change how you communicate in future relationships. It is my view that the only reason why we are romantically attracted to each other in the first place is for soul growth. Our partner is in our life to hold a mirror up to us and show us our unresolved issues. We can either accept and address those issues with accountability and evolve or we can remain a victim of our circumstances and stay stuck in repeating patterns. The choice is ours.

Chapter 4

What to Expect during the Divorce Process

R*eptilian Brain*

Divorce is one of life's greatest tragedies. It's second only to the death of a close friend or family member in terms of the grieving process. When you are grieving, you are vulnerable and not as emotionally regulated as you might be otherwise. Combine the grief with fear of the unknown and anxiety about your future and you have a hot mess. When you are triggered, and your spouse is likely your biggest trigger right now, sometimes you become angry and reactive. You might be irritable and impatient with your children and other loved ones in your life. When you are in this state, it can feel as though you have no control over your emotions. In order to gain some control, it's helpful to understand at a high level how the brain functions in times of crisis.

For the purposes of this exercise, it's helpful to use your hand to understand the brain. Dr. Dan Siegel, MD who is an expert on neurobiology has written many books on how the brain functions. He also has a YouTube video to demonstrate how to use your hand as a model for the brain https://www.youtube.com/watch?v=f-m2YcdMdFw&t=318s. If you have an interest in learning more about brain functioning, I highly recommend his work.

With your hand, fold your fingers over your thumb and make a fist. The thumb, now buried under your fingers, represents the limbic region of the brain. Your fingers represent the prefrontal cortex region. Your wrist is the brain stem. When you get triggered, the limbic system, the more impulsive part of the brain...the thumb, gets activated and "hijacks" the logical part of the brain, the fingers. The limbic system connects to the brain stem, also known as the reptilian brain, because it's the oldest part of the brain, which is connected to the spinal column, thus affecting your body's response to emotion and trauma. Since the cortex is now functioning in the background, you aren't making logical choices. You become more reactive, you will say and do things you can't unsay or undo. The good news is, there are ways of managing this response if you are proactive.

Separating the Emotions of Divorce from the Business of Divorce, The Grieving Process

First of all, it's important to separate the emotions of divorce from the business of divorce. You are going to feel vulnerable and emotional so just accept it...it is a normal response to a transition of this magnitude. What we resist persists. Then, identify what specifically are your triggers and how you respond physically to them. I have a short exercise I do with my clients that helps you gain some perspective. This exercise is from the model of therapy called Rational Emotive Behavior Therapy (REBT). REBT, created by Dr. Albert Ellis in 1955, helps create awareness around how our thoughts, specifically the stories we make up in our head, determine what we believe about our circumstances. Once you become aware of the thoughts, you can change them, thus changing your beliefs about your circumstances. I often preface this exercise with my clients by stressing "you can't have a positive life with a negative mind."

I have a worksheet available for free on the homepage my website https://divorceresiliency.com but in case you don't have access to the internet, on a blank piece of paper (landscape) write across the bottom A (activating event, aka the trigger for your anxiety), B (the underlying belief about the trigger, aka racing thoughts or stories you are creating about the trigger) and C (the consequence, or how the anxiety makes you feel physically). Over the "A" write the thing that is triggering your anxiety. Let's use the example of "my ex-husband doesn't respond to my texts." Then go to the "C" column and list how your body is responding to the trigger. Examples: tense, tearful, rapid breathing, heart pounding, poor focus, poor sleep, poor appetite, etc. Finally, go to the "B" column. This is where you will list the thoughts that are ramping up the emotion (the "motor" for the C column so to speak). Using our example, here are some thoughts that might correspond:

- He is ignoring me in order to manipulate me
- He is dating someone else
- He is always trying to make me angry
- He doesn't care about me and is over there having a blast
- He's dead on the side of the road
- He doesn't care about our children
- He's setting me up to not follow through on his obligations
- Why did I ever marry that man?
- I obviously have never known how to pick men
- I'm just not lovable

These are called negative cognitions (thought patterns). They typically start with one negative thought and snowball. When doing this exercise and writing in the "B" column, it's very important not to censor or judge yourself. Just let it be a stream of consciousness. Get it all out. Use swear words if you must. Once you have it all out, notice what is going on in your body. Are you feeling some of the physical sensations listed in the "C" column? Congratulations! You now recognize how your brain affects your body and emotions. There is a connection! Once you figure this out, you see that with your thoughts you have some control over your emotions.

The first thing you want to do is soothe and nurture yourself. Having the ability to self-soothe is crucial in managing our emotions. You are grieving right now and in the birth canal. The only way out of grief is through it. If you allow yourself to feel it, you might experience some personal growth in the process. According to Elisabeth Kubler-Ross, there are five stages of grief: 1) anger, 2) denial, 3) bargaining, 4) depression, 5) acceptance. These stages can include a wide range of emotions and don't always come in order. Some of them can occur simultaneously! If you are tearful, draw a bath, light some candles and cry it out in the tub. Maybe watch a sad movie or listen to music to connect with your grief. If you are angry, scream into a pillow or throw some ice cubes into a tub of water. Take an ax-throwing class or sign up for a plate throwing session. Take a kick-boxing class or put a picture of your spouse on a punching bag and punch until you are spent. Put a picture of your spouse in a chair and scream at it. Don't censor yourself! Let the 4-letter words flow freely. If you are anxious with rapid breathing, do some deep breathing exercises or take a walk outside (the more you are surrounded by nature the better). If you can and weather permits, put your bare feet on the earth (a technique called "grounding"). Hug a tree. Sometimes if I'm walking a nature trail and I need to feel more grounded but don't want others to see me hugging a tree, I'll just lean my back against one and feign looking at my phone. It works! You can also sit on the ground with your back against the tree.

A meditation and/or yoga practice can help you proactively manage your emotions. There is new research coming out all the time about how mindfulness activities have an impact on the mind and body in a positive way. Yoga, in particular, helps bring the brain and body into balance. Journaling is an excellent way to get all the emotion out. Again, don't censor or judge yourself. I have a daily journaling practice and recommend it to all my clients. At the end of each entry, set an intention and make a gratitude list so you end on a positive note. You can download a free diary app to your tablet and assign a password so your thoughts are kept safe from prying eyes.

These are just a few examples of how you can nurture yourself. In general, you want to use healthy coping mechanisms right now. It's crucial not to "stuff" your emotions, self-medicate or deny that you are feeling them. All that does is prolong the grieving process. When you ignore or "stuff" your negative feelings, they don't go away, they just show up in other, unhealthy ways (such as drinking too much, exercising too much, eating too much or too little, etc). Many people distract themselves from their negative thoughts by trying to stay busy. It's important to allow yourself to sit with your negative emotions and fully experience them. Really living is about experiencing a full range of emotions.

Getting Unstuck and Managing the Overwhelm

Once you are in a calmer, more grounded and present place, go back and look at the list of thoughts. There are typically 4 themes:

1. Creating negative predictions or stories around an unknown future
2. Regrets about past decisions that you can't change
3. "Othering" (focusing on others' thoughts, feelings and behaviors that you can't control and creating stories around them)
4. Extreme thinking, "awfulizing" or "catastrophizing" ("I'm always going to be alone", "I never have a voice", "My life is terrible", etc).

Now, go through your list of thoughts and write beside each one the corresponding number. You'll find some thoughts have more than one number. Can you see now how you not only beat yourself up with your thoughts but keep yourself out of the present moment? It's also pretty clear why you are feeling overwhelmed.

I find that my clients typically have one or two "go-to" thought patterns. Knowing yours can help you gain some control over them. Ask yourself the following questions: What is within my control? What is based in-fact as I know it right now? Is there evidence against what I am thinking? What would a rational friend or family member say about this thought? What action can I take, right now, to improve this situation? What thought honors the highest and best version of myself?

The good news is that this is going to pass. You won't feel this way forever, but if you can catch yourself when you are going down the rabbit hole with your thoughts, you can reign them in. The key is to try to keep your thoughts reality-based and on what you can control. Focus on the here and now. You will have moments when you are more successful at this than others, but that's okay. Above all, be kind to yourself and forgive yourself. You are not operating from your best self right now but you WILL get back there. You will have some days where you feel you are making progress and some days where you feel you have had a setback. But generally speaking, with each passing month it gets a little better. Having said this, in the early stages sometimes it gets worse before it gets better. Once you start to shift your thinking to what you can control and away from what you can't you start to become less overwhelmed and can make decisions that will help move your forward and become "unstuck".

Managing Conflict with your Spouse

Now that you have some techniques to understand your triggers and manage your emotions, let's talk for a bit about communicating with your ex in a more effective way. Make a list of the things he does that just drives you nuts. Now, look at the list and say to yourself "I can't do anything to change this...not a damn thing!" What you CAN do, however, is control how you respond to him. If you need to resort to strictly electronic communication, so be it. Email and text communication give you time to process your triggers then respond when you have had some time to think through your response. If you need to speak to him over the phone, write down your thoughts prior to the conversation and take notes as he is speaking to keep yourself in the logical part of the brain. If he tries to bait you, and I'm sure you know what that looks like, DON'T TAKE THE BAIT!!! I cannot stress this enough.

Bill Eddy, an expert on high conflict personalities, has a technique called BIFF which stands for Brief, Informative, Friendly, and Firm. He describes this technique in his book "BIFF: Quick Responses to High-Conflict People, Their Personal Attacks, Hostile Email and Social Media Meltdowns" (Eddy, 2014) . There is a YouTube video by Tess Brook of Cohesive Conversations where she is interviewing Bill Eddy https://www.youtube.com/watch?v=4V7ZAZ8SJxU describing this technique if you'd like to explore in more detail. Essentially, Eddy suggests you respond in a friendly, fact-based, future-focused kind of way. There is no need at this point to rehash old stuff or allow your ex to dump his negative cognitions on you. He's dealing with his own triggers but you don't have to respond to them. Take the high road! This is much easier if you are acknowledging and using techniques to manage your own overwhelm and emotions.

Effective Relationship with Your Attorney/Saving Money in Divorce

For those of you who are in the midst of the legal process of your divorce, you can use these techniques to manage your emotions so you aren't using your attorney as your therapist. Your attorney is not equipped to manage the emotional process of your divorce. Their role is to manage the business of your divorce. I often find that fear takes over with my clients and they fill up their attorney's voicemail and email from this fearful place. Using your attorney as your therapist not only frustrates your attorney, but it drives up the cost of the divorce. Using a therapist and/or a divorce coach who is experienced and knowledgeable about all the fearful emotions that can come up during divorce is incredibly helpful.

Team of Support

A divorce coach is a relatively new phenomenon. I'm often asked what is the difference between a divorce coach and a therapist. A therapist is equipped to assist you in healing any negative relationship patterns that are rooted in childhood trauma and may be affecting your relationships as an adult. A coach works with you on the divorce process in the here and now and can help you move forward efficiently by helping you manage your emotions during that process. Not only can they help you with resources for forming your team of support, but they operate as a thinking and accountability partner to help you from getting stuck in the overwhelm. Anyone can put themselves out there as a divorce coach, but, ideally, it's best to use a CDC Certified Divorce Coach® (https://certifieddivorcecoach.com/) because of the rigorous training process, continuing education requirement and board of standards.

As I stated previously in this chapter, using your attorney as an emotional dumpster just drives up the cost and typically isn't effective. If you don't want to use a therapist or coach, join a divorce support group. If you can't find one that a therapist runs, many local churches have them. Divore Care https://www.divorcecare.org/ is a popular group/class that many churches will sponsor. Meetup https://www.meetup.com/ is another resource for finding meet-up groups for separated and divorced individuals. I find groups that are gender specific tend to provide a safer environment earlier on in the divorce journey, although mixed gender groups, if they are run well with clear boundaries, can be good options. If you can't afford individual therapy, group therapy can be a wonderful alternative.

For some women, the possible loss of financial security can feel overwhelming and be a big trigger. This is a good time to hire a Certified Divorce Financial Analyst (CDFA®) to help with the financial part of your divorce. A CDFA® can not only help you make sense of your finances but help you plan for your financial future.

Divorce can provide a great opportunity to gain clarity around your finances and set financial goals that are individual to you. Having a sense of your financial landscape can also be grounding. If you use a financial planner without CDFA® training, some financial issues that apply specifically in divorce might get missed. CDFA®s are considered financial neutrals and can work with both you and your former spouse to come up with an equitable split during the divorce process. If you don't feel you have enough assets to retain the expertise of a professional, Dave Ramsey has a wonderful, easy to follow program outlined in his book "The Total Money Makeover" (2013). He also has a podcast and Facebook group to help reinforce his message and keep you motivated to stay on track with your goals.

Having a team of experts who are skilled at handling clients going through divorce can help keep you grounded and logical at this time. Along with your team of experts, surrounding yourself with peers who share your experience can be a powerful remedy. I found when I was going through my own divorce and have witnessed the same with my clients in the support group I run, how soothing it can feel to be with others who are going through the same thing and experiencing the same emotions. There is a special healing energy that occurs in my groups that is hard to describe. Many of the women in my groups form friendships and continue to meet after the formal group ends. It's incredibly difficult to navigate a divorce on your own and you'll need a team of support around you.

Chapter 5

What About the Kids?
Co-Parenting Skills

Usually when I first see a client, they are experiencing what I refer to as relationship ambiguity. They have been unhappy in their marriage for a while and are seriously considering divorce. In most cases, when there are kids involved, my clients will state that they would already be out of the marriage if they didn't have children. People will stay in unhappy marriages for years because of their children. Although I don't have children, I empathize with why this can be agonizing based on my own childhood experience. My mother stayed in her marriage to my father for much longer than she should have while waiting for me to graduate from high school. She didn't quite make it.

In a study conducted in the year 2000 by Dr. Stephen Josephs, PhD and his colleagues of 400 young teens on common life-threatening events that can cause PTSD, 29% of boys and 39% of girls reported PTSD symptoms post-divorce. This is due to HOW the divorce was handled, not the divorce itself. Having said this, it is also traumatizing for children to live in households with two parents who are unhappy, no longer loving with each other and can't get along. As I can personally attest, exposing the children to ongoing dysfunction is not doing them any favors. If a marriage is irreparable, it is best for the children that you both be happy, fulfilled, united co-parents.

Kids in general thrive on routine and structure. In chapter 1 I discussed attachment styles. Children generally like to know what to expect and function best in a loving, stable environment where they are free to be kids. This type of environment breeds a secure attachment style. Staying in an unhappy marriage where emotional disconnect, unhealthy conflict is being modeled, or there is physical or emotional unavailability, or worse, abuse and neglect does not ensure a secure attachment style. So how do you provide a stable environment from two households? By becoming joined and united with the other parent in co-parenting. This is where it is helpful to separate your partner's role as a parent vs. a spouse. This is sometimes difficult to accomplish early on in the divorce process when emotions are high, but is very possible and attainable once the dust settles.

The research shows it can take up to three years to adjust to a divorce for the whole family, but especially for the kids. The first year is usually about "what the heck just happened", year 2 is "how do we fix what we did wrong in year 1", and year 3 is "lets get settled into these new patterns." This timeline is determined by how well you and your former spouse transition into co-parenting roles. Following a few simple guidelines can help with this transition.

Please keep in mind that the information provided here is assuming both parents are well-adjusted with the normal emotional ups and downs that come with divorce. If you are dealing with a mentally ill spouse, with a personality disorder such as Narcissistic Personality Disorder (NPD) or Borderline Personality Disorder (BPD), or a spouse who is in active alcoholism or addiction, immediately consult with a therapist. If you feel you and/or your children are in danger, please contact the Domestic Violence Hotline 800-799-7233 or local law enforcement.

This information is pulled not only from my training as a marriage and family therapist and Certified Divorce Coach® and also from the experience of my clients. Generally speaking, the younger the child, the easier it is for them to adjust. Teenagers tend to have the most difficulty adjusting. I once worked with a 6-year old little girl whose parents were divorced when she was 2-years old. I asked her if she remembered a time when her parents were living together. She said "ooo no! That would be so weird!." Her mom was so worried that she was suffering and, not only did she not remember the divorce, but she had grown adjusted to having parents who lived apart.

Assuming you do everything right on your end, you can make it easier for your children. Having said this, you're human and may make some mistakes. Try to learn from them and adjust as you move along. As I have said previously, most of the trauma for kids lies in how YOU and YOUR SPOUSE handle the divorce, not in the divorce itself. It is crucial that you both attempt to keep your sights set on your children and focus on them as you move forward in your divorce journey. This is much easier to do once you reach the acceptance phase of grief. In general, you must love your kids MORE than you dis-like (and in some cases hate) your spouse.

In chapter 1 I discuss methods to stay in the logical part of your brain. Those same methods apply here. You want to do the best you can to stay logical and grounded as you move forward...this is easier said than done when dealing with a life transition of this magnitude. Recognize when you are feeling triggered or emotionally flooded and don't react at that moment. Calm yourself down before you respond to your spouse, even if that means taking a break from each other. Don't bait each other into an argument and don't take the bait. Always, always, always take the high road in communication. Try to see their perspective and take some ownership in discussions. Sometimes, early on in the process, keeping your communication over email or text gives you time to process your emotions before you respond. Working with a coach/therapist can help. Remember, things said can't be unsaid and actions can't be reversed. If you can get through this with a good co-parenting relationship intact, it will have a positive impact on the next phase of your life. I'll provide some specific communication techniques later on in this book.

For all children, keeping their routine and structure as stable as possible is incredibly helpful. Not only do infants and toddlers thrive in routine, but older children do as well. Once a child reaches pre-teen years, you can be more flexible. It's best if both parents can maintain a united front with the children when it comes to parenting. Co-parents should talk through a parenting plan with rewards and punishments proactively so they are both on the same page. You can enlist the help of a co-parenting therapist if you need a 3rd party to help facilitate the conversation. If a child is in the custody of one parent who disciplines the child by taking away a privilege (e.g. use of their tablet or phone has been taken away), it's best for the other parent to resume this discipline when the child is returned to their custody. If there are any pets, it's best for them to go with the child back and forth between the homes (assuming the pet can adjust to the different environments). It's also best for each home to have everything the child needs so he/she doesn't have to pack a bag every time they change custody. Keep the same sleep schedule as well as school/homework schedule and play time. Children want to be reassured their world isn't going to change so try to keep it as consistent as possible among households. Keep lines of communication open and fluid. Don't ever use your children to communicate with each other. If children sense that you two aren't united, in some cases, they will use it to their advantage. It also causes them anxiety and stress. If you aren't able to get along and present a united front when attending school, sporting events or extracurricular activities then alternate attending them when the child is in your custody. Children will sense how divided you are and will be focusing on the awkwardness around that vs. the activity. Children are incredibly intuitive and likely pick up on more dysfunction than you think they do.

When speaking about the other parent, do so in positive terms, or don't say anything. Although it might be tempting to "bad talk" the other parent so you look better in the eyes of the child, all this does is cause the child stress. This applies to children of any age, including adult children. Remember, they have the other parent's blood and DNA in their bodies and will feel conflicted when they hear you speak poorly about the other parent. This same rule also applies when you tell your child "you're just like your father/mother" as a form of criticism in a fit of anger. Instead, try to keep your comments about the other parent positive or neutral. For example, when the child is going to see the other parent say something to the effect of "aren't you excited!? You get to go see your father today!", or "I love hearing you play the guitar. You're so talented. You got your musical abilities from your father."

You also want to be aware of any red flags. Oftentimes, kids blame themselves for the divorce. When a child is feeling stressed, it will likely show up as unusual behavior issues. Be aware of the following signs of stress:

1. isolation
2. poor hygiene
3. acting out, aggressive behavior
4. no longer wanting to do what they normally like to do
5. issues at school and with grades.

A child's prefrontal cortex, the area of logical functioning in the brain, is not fully developed until they are in their 20s. It is your role as a parent to be a logical presence and guide them. Try not to react to what is being presented by the child, try instead to get to the root issue, which is likely a vulnerability. You can do this by showing empathy for the child and reflecting back to them their emotions "you must be feeling sad today" or "you seem angry about something". Validate what they are feeling. Never ever ever tell them what they are feeling is wrong. Get them into therapy so they can have a safe place to discuss their feelings. Sometimes they don't want to share with the parent because they don't want to cause any additional burden to them. The best thing you can do for your children is regularly carve out some one-on-one time with them with no distractions (no TV or devices) and allow them to dictate what they want to do and/ or discuss or how they want to play during this time. Don't try to direct them, but just be present with them as they do all the directing.

I'm sure there are many of you out there who are reading this and thinking "I have tried everything, my ex just won't co-parent with me!" In some cases, you even question his abilities to parent in general. Be assured that if you are providing a loving, secure base as described above with your child where there's good routine and structure and your child feels safe to be a kid, it will offset much if any damage that is being done by the other parent. Remember, you can't change him, you can only change you! If you genuinely feel that your child is unsafe with the other parent, and aren't creating stories in your head about this, then document, document, document. The documentation can help should you end up back in court.

Disney Dad

When a couple divorces and moves into their custody arrangement, I'll occasionally have a client who will express frustration over the fact that the children come home from their father's custody with breathless enthusiasm, eager to share all the fun trips and activities they did when they were in his care. The frustration comes from the fact that, oftentimes, when the marriage was still intact, the father was checked out and didn't co-parent well and the brunt of the structure and discipline fell on the mother (and still does post-separation). In addition, perhaps when the family unit was still intact, Mom had to plan and put all the effort into making sure the trips and activities happened with little to no help from her spouse. In some cases, post-separation, there is a big difference in income and the father has the financial means to plan these activities, when the mother isn't able to afford them.

These Dads are often referred to as "Disney Dads", because they seem to want to be "fun Dad" and not partake in the heavy-lifting that comes with parenting. If this describes your situation, I encourage you to think about how your children interact with you. Who is the one they call when they fall off the bike and hurt their knee? Who is the parent they confide in most often? Who provides a secure base for them? Disney Dads often don't know how to parent, so they create these fun activities as a way to continue to be "checked-out" and not have to deal with their child's negative emotions with divorce.

I can remember during one of own my parents' separations when I was about 7-years old, my father was a Disney Dad. I can remember him giving us elaborate presents, taking us out to eat wherever we wanted and having yummy name brand goodies in the house when all my Mom could afford was the store brand. As an adult looking back on this time, I'm sure my mother's heart was broken that she couldn't provide for us in the same way. But she was a wonderful confidante and the first one I called when I needed a sympathetic ear, all the way to the end of her life.

When it comes to co-parenting, there are many pitfalls that could pop up. As long as you are willing to work on how you show up in the relationship with your ex-husband and unwind from any negative, codependent patterns that existed while you were still married to him, a repair is possible. You may have to accept certain qualities about him that aren't able to be changed. Afterall, a zebra can't change his stripes. But you can change how you communicate with him. Sometimes it's best to let go of the reins and let their father figure out how to handle certain challenging situations when they are in his custody without your input. For older children, let them navigate their relationship with their father. It will have a long lasting impact on how they advocate for themselves in their lives with various personalities that will cross their paths in their lifetime.

As much as you may want to disassociate from your spouse when you divorce him, when you had children with him you signed on for a parenting relationship for life. Getting it right early on will determine how easy this transition will be for everyone.

Chapter 6

Unwinding from Codependency with Healthy Boundaries

As I mentioned in Chapter 1, we define much of our identity from "being married." We create a narrative around our married life and then become the narrative. It defines us. When we divorce the narrative suddenly changes and we feel lost trying to figure out the new normal for ourselves. This process of trying to figure out who we are on our own can feel not only scary but overwhelming. Many people, when feeling overwhelmed, feel some relief by sharing their angst with others. I remember when I was going through my divorce and would meet any random stranger, I would introduce myself as "Hi, I'm Sherry, and I'm going through a divorce". It consumed me and was all I could think about.

Children, in particular, depending on their age, might feel like a source of support for you because they know the story and their parents better than anyone. It is very tempting to overshare with them. Please keep in mind that these are adult issues and more than a child should be required to handle. No matter how mature your child might be, it's crucial to have healthy boundaries with them during this time. Even if they seem mature, as described earlier in this book, their brains are not fully developed biologically and they aren't developmentally ready to handle your emotions. Even with adult children, when oversharing our side of the story, puts the children in an awkward position of feeling they need to pick sides.

The same applies for friends, family members and colleagues. Although it's helpful to have a few close friends or family members who you feel you can depend on as a source of support, you don't want to overwhelm them with your emotions. They most likely aren't equipped with how to handle your situation. Many people feel anxious when someone they are close to is feeling vulnerable and feel the need to "fix it" as a way to soothe their own anxiety. In many cases, advice is not what you are seeking, and it very possibly could be bad advice! This can cause conflict in the relationship.

Julia had been in an unhappy marriage for years. She even questioned if she really loved her husband when they got married. As soon as her marriage ended, she felt overwhelmed and confused about what the next chapter was going to look like for her. She immediately got involved with a man from her gym, Steve, who was inappropriate for her. She fell head over heels for Steve even though he was evasive and sometimes non-responsive. He made it clear to her that he wasn't ready for a relationship, but Julia was convinced he would eventually realize his feelings for her and commit. At the same time, Julia was also feeling conflicted over whether it was right to end her marriage. When she went out with her friends, the conversation was consumed with her angst over her divorce as well as her relationship with Steve. She spent countless hours analyzing Steve's motives, making up stories in her head about what his real intentions were and whether he was dating other women. She started to lose friends because they were becoming exhausted from her obsession with Steve and indecision about her marriage.

Julia was aware that she couldn't stop talking about her circumstances and was becoming a burden. She even acknowledged that she didn't even like herself sometimes! Julia felt she had little control over her life. She could feel her self-esteem slipping away and eventually landed in my office. In our work together, she figured out that she actually did have some control over what she was allowing in her life. She did some work on her codependent patterns and focused on what was within her control, such as advancing her career and developing some hobbies. She worked on using her voice in a healthy and balanced way in all her relationships. She worked on salvaging her relationships with her friends, who were very valuable to her. It took her a while, but she was eventually strong enough to end her relationship with Steve and get clear that she didn't love her husband and he should be free to move on. Once she was clear about these things, she was able to focus on herself for a while.

Codependency is not the opposite of being independent as people often think. I have had more than one client say, "I can't be codependent, I'm an independent woman!" You can be a self-sufficient, independent woman but still have codependent patterns in your relationships. In fact, I find that my clients who were parentified as children are the most high achieving and independent adults. They are also the most codependent in their relationships due to their need to control their environment, something they learned was necessary as a child for their very survival.

Codependency is often rooted in childhood trauma or it could have been modeled for us by our parents even if we had a relatively safe environment growing up. According to Darlene Lancer, JD, MFT, "codependency is characterized by a person belonging to a dysfunctional, one-sided relationship where one person relies on the other for meeting nearly all of their emotional and self-esteem needs. It also describes a relationship that enables another person to maintain their irresponsible, addictive, or underachieving behavior" (2018). Two pioneers of the concept of codependency are Melodie Beattie, author of "Codependent No-More" (1986) and Pia Melody "Facing Codependence" (2003). Both of these women came from the recovery arena and use recovery language in their books. I recommend them often to help clients recognize their own codependent patterns.

Julia's example above demonstrates how codependency can be all-consuming and unhealthy. It is exhausting to own and try to control everyone else's thoughts, feelings and behaviors. People pleasers fall in the codependency camp as well. If you are a people pleaser or feel the need to take on the roles and responsibilities of others, feel the need to control others to manage your anxiety, or feel you can anticipate and fulfill other's needs for them, and later, feel resentment, guess what? You are codependent.

When discussing the concept of codependency with my clients, I often hear "I don't want to be mean", or "I don't want to hurt his/ her feelings." Speaking your truth is actually more kind in the long run because you are being honest with yourself and the other person. As you get more practice, you will learn it can be done in a kind and compassionate way. Having said this, in the early days of practicing this you may "overshoot" by being too harsh. I would rather you be too harsh than not be honest. In time, you'll get better at communicating from this authentic place.

The way to unwind from codependent patterns is with boundaries and owning your own "stuff" while letting go of other people's "stuff". Let them control what is in their wheelhouse and you control what is in your wheelhouse. I heard this description of codependency one time and use it often...being a supportive friend means walking beside them on their path. Being a codependent friend is carrying them on your back.

Boundaries are established through clear communication. It's important to let the people you choose to lean on know what you need from them. Are you looking for advice or do you just need to be heard? You might ask them to let you know if they are feeling overwhelmed and need a break from discussing the divorce. It's also crucial to have balance in your life. It's healthy to redirect your thoughts to other things and friends can be a great resource for this. I personally sometimes really enjoy going out with my friends and talking about fashion or the latest celebrity gossip. It's a wonderful distraction from being in therapeutic-mode all day!

Having said this, you do need a healthy outlet to talk about your circumstances. This is another reason why a divorce support group can be helpful or enlisting the help of a therapist or divorce coach where you can have a safe place to vent and express your emotions. Surround yourself with people who are going through or have been divorced who can relate to your experience. Starting a journaling practice where you are free to be completely honest about what you are feeling can help get the thoughts out of your head and onto the page. I find I can't sleep at night without journaling before I go to bed! It is a practice I have enjoyed for more than 10 years. I particularly enjoy looking back at previous entries to see where I was then versus now.

Many of my clients worry about the news of their divorce getting out before they are ready to talk about the fact that their marriage is ending. They concern themselves with how to tell people and want help with right dialogue. It's crucial for you to be aware, you are in charge of your own story. You can control the narrative to a certain degree. You can choose when you want to tell people. Having said this, yes, the word might spread once you start to tell a few people. I find it helpful to come up with a high-level version of the story that you want to share with people who are acquaintances and a more detailed version of the story that is for people who are closer to you. For example, if you run into a neighbor in the grocery story who boldly offers her concern because she has heard you are getting divorced, you might say, "I can confirm that what you have heard is correct, but I'm not quite ready to discuss it yet. I hope you understand" or you might say "I'm focusing my energy on protecting my children right now as we move through this difficult transition and am not quite ready to discuss the details of our circumstances right now." If the person you are talking to is a family member or friend, you may choose to give more details. I recommend you use as much "we" or "I" language as possible and try to keep it neutral without pointing fingers. You want to look back on how you handled this time in your life and feel proud of yourself.

Chapter 7

Trauma Bonding and Rewiring Neural Pathways in the Brain

Historically it was believed that the brain we were born with was the brain we were stuck with our whole life. New research is showing that the brain has neuroplasticity, meaning it is more flexible than we previously believed. The definition of neuroplasticity is "the brain's ability to reorganize itself by forming new neural connections throughout life. Neuroplasticity allows the neurons (nerve cells) in the brain to compensate for injury and disease and to adjust their activities in response to new situations or to changes in their environment." (Shiel, n.d.).

According to Duboc (n.d.) "Every time you learn something, neural circuits are altered in your brain. These circuits are composed of a number of neurons (nerve cells) that communicate with one another through special junctions called synapses." When learning any new activity, a new word or new behavior, you are training your brain to create new neural pathways.

When understanding the brain's neuroplasticity, it is clear to see how certain events or circumstances can affect the brain's wiring. Especially in the case of repeated events, such as abuse. This is especially true when experiencing a destructive childhood environment when chaos is happening while a child's brain is developing. This chaos can literally affect the brain's development. This upbringing can manifest later in life by trauma bonding with an abusive partner.

Patrick Carnes, PhD introduced the concept of trauma bonding in his book "The Betrayal Bond". According to Dr. Carnes (2019), following are signs of trauma bonding:

1. When everyone around the client is having negative reactions so strong the client is covering up, defending, or explaining a relationship.
2. When there is a constant pattern of non-performance and the client continues to expect them to follow through anyway.
3. When there are repetitive, destructive fights that are no win for anybody.
4. When others are horrified by something that has happened to the client and the client isn't.
5. When the client obsesses about showing someone that they are wrong about the abuse, their relationship, or their treatment of the client.
6. When the client feels loyal to someone even though the client harbors secrets that are damaging to others.
7. When the client moves closer to someone who is destructive with the desire of converting them to a non-abuser.
8. When someone's talents, charisma, or contributions causes the client to overlook destructive, exploitive, or degrading acts.
9. When the client cannot detach from someone even though the client does not trust, like or care for the person.
10. When the client misses a relationship even to the point of nostalgia and longing that was so awful it almost destroyed the client.
11. When extraordinary demands are placed on the client to measure up as a way to cover up exploitation of the client.
12. When the client keeps secret someone's destructive behavior because of all of the good they have done or the importance of their position or career.
13. When the history of their relationship is about contracts or

promises that have been broken, which the client is asked to overlook.

Sharon was a client of mine who was the most dedicated to keeping a journal. When her appointment time would arrive and I would come to collect her from the lobby, she would be bent over her journal writing furiously. She would share entries in session and said that she gained amazing self-awareness and insight from her entries. Sharon came to me when she was thinking about leaving her marriage to a self-identified narcissist, which she said in her first session had been unhappy for at least a decade. Sharon said she struggled with poor self-esteem and in-session would beat herself up with her constant negative self-talk.

In our work together, Sharon finally admitted to herself that her unhappiness spanned the life of her marriage, not just the last decade. She realized she married for more logical reasons to escape her chaotic home environment. She felt she had never had an emotional or physical connection with her husband. She admitted to never having an orgasm when they had sex. Now in her 50's, and with her children grown and out of the house, Sharon embarked on a long period of self-discovery. I was awed and inspired by her ability to be completely honest with herself and the circumstances that led to her making the decisions that got her to this place in her life.

About 2-months into our work together, Sharon disclosed that she had been sexually abused as a child from the ages of 6 until 14-years old. Her home life was chaotic and she never felt safe or protected so she left home at the age of 16. She married at 19-years old to her current husband, Bruce, a much older man of 30-years old who, she thought, would provide a secure life and be a good provider. Her husband was an Ivy League graduate with an advanced degree and had embarked on what would eventually become a successful, financially lucrative career as an investment banker.

Sharon admitted that there were red flags when she was dating her husband and that, even then, he was selfish and emotionally abusive. He would laugh when she tried to express her needs, make fun of her and insult her in front of other people, and threaten her if she didn't behave or dress the way he wanted her to or associate with people who were of his liking. He would joke that he was a narcissist, almost as if he was proud of it. Early in her marriage, Bruce would apologize and buy her gifts when he felt remorse from abusing her. This making amends stopped later in their marriage. Sharon admitted that outwardly her family presented as a perfect family of wealth and privilege while inside she felt lonely and isolated, as if her identity and self-esteem had melted away. Everyone who was close to her questioned why she stayed in her marriage.

Sharon had never disclosed her childhood sexual abuse to anyone before, not even her husband. Because she shared this with me, we were able to work on the trauma using EMDR https://www.emdr. com/what-is-emdr/, an effective model of therapy to help rewire the brain's neural pathways. Through this work she was able to see how her childhood trauma had impacted her decisions throughout her life. She didn't realize how much she was blaming herself and carrying shame because of poor decisions she had made. When she made the link between the childhood trauma and her decision-making she was finally able to forgive herself. She was then able to exit her marriage while remaining emotionally regulated, thus allowing for a more amicable divorce. Eventually, she was able to accept her husband for who he is and treat him with more compassion. She took the high road in all of their interactions.

When Sharon first came to me, she blamed her husband for her unhappiness. She was a victim as a child and continued to be a victim as an adult. By the time we were done, she was not only more empowered, but living a happier life. The last time I saw her, she happily reported she was seeing a man who was kind, compassionate, loving and considerate of her needs. For the first time in her life, she had a happy, healthy relationship with a man who not only loved her, but also loved her children! Because she worked on herself, she was able to "fix her picker" and make a better decision, choosing a better partner the second time around. She said her life was better than she ever imagined it could be!

When we experience trauma of this magnitude, neural pathways are formed in the brain affecting not only how we make decisions but also how we respond to certain events in our lives. When that trauma goes unprocessed, it can seem as though life is difficult. Because it can seem as though bad things frequently happen to us, we can go through life viewing everything through a fearful, anxious lens feeling tense and hypervigilant as if we are anticipating the next negative experience. According to Loder (2015) "Here's the good news: with training, scientists have now shown, we can literally rewire the neural pathways that regulate our emotions, thoughts, and reactions. This means we can create new neural pathways - highways in our brain - that lead us to compassion, gratitude, and joy instead of anxiety, fear, and anger." This can be accomplished with the help of a licensed therapist using EMDR, but can also be achieved by simply practicing compassion.

I am going to recommend an exercise that will help you focus your compassion in a productive way to help with reprogramming your own neural pathways. This exercise can be used in a variety of relationships, but I'm going to use it in the context of divorce.

Everytime you find yourself angry at your ex, either by something he has said or has done or by remembering past events where you felt wronged, I suggest you redirect your attention to your heart. Imagine a color there that represents love, peace and healing. Now imagine your ex-husband bathed in that light. You might even imagine him doing an activity that he loves while feeling pure joy and peace as he is surrounded by this light. If you don't know of an activity he enjoys, just imagine him sitting in the light feeling it's warmth and healing energy. You might even imagine a giant smile on his face. Now, notice how you feel as you imagine this. Do you feel more anger and resistance or do you also feel some peace? If you feel resistance and anger, ask yourself what that is about? Resist the urge to turn the anger back on him. Ask yourself, what is the anger telling you about yourself? Anger is always a mask for the soft underbelly of vulnerability. What is the vulnerability that your anger is protecting? The more honest with yourself you are about this, the easier this exercise becomes. Why is that, you ask? Because not only are you sending him healing light and intention, but you are doing the same for yourself!

Continue with this exercise everytime you feel angry towards him. Over time, if you are diligent with the exercise, you should actually stop feeling angry and start to feel more neutral towards him. You may actually start to feel compassion for him.

Chapter 8

Blended Family Structure

As I indicated in chapter 5, it is imperative that you and your former spouse present a joined and united front when co-parenting your children. I recently read an Instagram post from supermodel Paulina Porizkova. The post originated when she and her husband initially split up and was shared again upon her husband's passing in 2019. Paulina was married to Ric Ocasek, one of the founders of the band The Cars. In the post, Paulina stated "Our family has always been — and still is — a well-built car. When the four of us are together, we can go wherever the road takes us. But as a bicycle, my husband and I no longer pedal in unison. So we're ditching the bicycle". Paulina was married to Ric for 28-years and had separated in 2017. It was no surprise to learn that she and her sons were with her former spouse at the time of his death, caring for him. This is the ideal structure for any family of divorce. Give yourself the opportunity to grieve the loss and get the other side of it so that you can become rejoined as co-parents to your children, the "'drivers' of the family car" so to speak. Kids can relax in this environment and enjoy the ride.

Having said this, the dynamic shifts when either or both of you decide to remarry. According to Pew Research Center (Livingston,

2014), the demographics of remarriage are as follows:

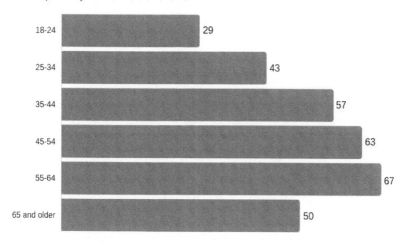

Remarriage by Age
% of the previously married who ever remarried

Age	Value
18-24	29
25-34	43
35-44	57
45-54	63
55-64	67
65 and older	50

Note: Previously married are those eligible for remarriage.

Source: Pew Research Center analysis of 2013 American Community Survey (1% IPUMS)

PEW RESEARCH CENTER

Based on this chart, the odds are very strong that your former spouse and/or you will remarry, so it's best to be prepared. In general, the research shows that the ideal blended family structure is for the bio-parents to be the rule-makers and create the structure, enforcing discipline with step-parents taking more of a subordinate role. Think more "adult friend" to the children, less "parent". I know what you're thinking…"he's impossible to reason with!" I hear you and validate you. But you still gotta navigate co-parenting with him. Get some help from a co-parenting therapist if necessary.

Stephanie was a client who came to me 4-years after her divorce was final. Both she and her ex-husband, Marco had remarried. Marco had been in and out of rehab on a regular basis for alcoholism. During their marriage not only was he drinking heavily, but he was cheating on her. The fighting was constant until Stephanie smartly realized she had to get herself and her children out of the chaos. After the divorce, when Marco no longer had an enabler, he hit bottom. He got into a 12-step program and obtained a therapist specializing in substance abuse. This combination worked for him and he was able to maintain some sobriety and obtain shared custody of his children. He quickly remarried to Renee, who had a long recovery in the same 12-step program that was a source of support for Marco. The fact that Marco remarried under these circumstances might elicit fear and panic in most women, but Stephanie was unique.

Stephanie, who by nature is a very mindful and spiritual person, established a friendship with Renee. They made an arrangement that if Marco was going through a bad time and shaky in his sobriety and it was his time to take custody of the kids, Renee would text Stephanie and just let her know it wasn't a good time for him to see the kids. Stephanie would ask no questions but would keep the children in her custody until she was given the green light by step-mom. Not only did this keep the children away from their father when he wasn't stable, but it forged a bond across caretakers that allowed them to attend the children's functions together and even take pictures together at these functions. The children are not only thriving, but have developed healthier coping skills. This is the ideal...and Stephanie had done a LOT of work on herself to get to this point before she even took a step into my office!

Now I'm going to ask you to get really honest with yourself. What does it feel like for you to think of the idea of a new maternal figure entering the picture with your children? Does it cause panic? Fear? Anxiety? Insecurity? Are you worried they are going to like her better than you? Do you fear that they are going to want to spend time with your ex-husband and his new wife over time with you? These are all thoughts and feelings my clients express on a regular basis. In fact, it's the exception, not the rule, that a new girlfriend or step-mom will NOT cause these feelings. I anticipate it with every one of my clients and they never disappoint. I challenge you, get ready for it. Because this is a HUGE part of your growth. The first step in that journey is to accept what you are feeling without judgement. What you resist persists!! Own it sister. What you don't want to do is try to create havoc in the dynamic in an effort to break them up.

Some clients will express a sense of satisfaction when their children won't speak to the new wife or misbehave in her presence. I assure you, although this might feel validating in the short term, this is NOT good for your children emotionally and is another sign of stress for them. Not only are they taking on "adult" feelings but they are feeling conflicted on where to place their loyalty. They are likely sensing your discomfort and siding with you. They are taking on the fight between you and your former spouse and no longer focusing on just being a kid.

Melissa came to me because she and her husband, Andrew, were fighting constantly, mostly over text, about his new girlfriend and how he chose to tell Melissa about his new relationship. They had been separated for 2-years and, up until then, had gotten along pretty well. Melissa stated in session that she had no interest in dating, but the agreement they had was that Andrew would let her know by text if and when he decided to date someone. Well, it didn't happen this way. Guess how she found out he was dating his college sweetheart? A prettier, younger version of Melissa? The woman she had heard about throughout her marriage and who was the one woman who could elicit jealousy? From her oldest son. Andrew had introduced his new girlfriend, Laura, to the children without Melissa being informed first. It didn't help that Andrew had lost the 50 lbs she had been nagging him about throughout their entire marriage. He was in the best shape of his life, and he did it for his new girlfriend.

In my work with Melissa, I helped her separate her feelings around the loss of the family versus her feelings for her husband. Once she was able to make this distinction, she was able to realize how her relationship with Andrew was codependent. Andrew was never fully present in their marriage and Melissa acknowledged that she questioned whether he ever really wanted to be married to her. Even when they were dating she felt insecure. Throughout their marriage, she vacillated between anticipating his needs and pleasing him to enabling and controlling him. She always felt like she wasn't "good enough" for him and felt she was constantly trying to present an ideal version of herself to please him so he wouldn't leave her for someone else. She realized how much not being authentic drained her energy. She had lost herself in her marriage.

When I asked Melissa about her hobbies and friends, she had none. She had no self-care routine. Every minute of her day was given to her Andrew and her children. Whose fault was that? Melissa's! When she was able to properly grieve the loss of the family unit, she realized she had already grieved the loss of her husband and actually felt liberated from their toxic dance.

Once Melissa was able to unwind from her codependency and show up for herself and others in a more authentic and healthy way, she started getting herself back. She saw how enmeshed she was with her children and how much she was leaning on them to meet her needs. She was able to step into the scary unknown and start meeting her own needs through changing careers, making new friends and developing some hobbies. She started nurturing herself with better nutrition and physical activity. She started a meditation practice and enjoyed it so much she found a group to meditate with. She got okay with saying "no" to people, made self-care more of a priority so she would be more grounded and present with her kids. We worked on how to communicate with Andrew by taking the high road and not taking the bait when he tried to draw her into an argument. She kept her communication future-focused, fact-based and set boundaries. Her children, who showed all the signs of stress by talking back, acting out and misbehaving, suddenly started to transform as well. She started getting her sweet kids back! Melissa not only got her groove back, but she lost 50 lbs herself! One year after becoming my client, she was able to meet Laura (by now engaged to Andrew) for coffee and start forging a relationship with her. Something that wouldn't have been possible for Melissa when she first found out about Laura. Melissa did the work and reaped the benefits and so did her kids.

I'm not going to lie, this work is hard! You have to be willing to face your demons and be vulnerable. The willingness to be honest with yourself and others about what you are feeling is the only way to show up for yourself and others in an authentic and healthy way. I get the benefit of seeing my client's courage to be vulnerable on a daily basis and it's amazing and inspiring to watch. I feel honored that they trust me enough to risk it. The beauty is that you are modeling vulnerability for your children while their brains are still developing... what a gift!

The ultimate goal is to provide a team of caretakers for your children so they benefit from having more love in their life. Charlotte, is a kind, empathic hairstylist with a love of the latest trends in clothing, make-up and hairstyles. Charlotte desperately wanted children of her own but was not able to have them with her first husband. She was thrilled at the idea of being a step-mom to David's three daughters from his previous marriage. Charlotte and David got married five years after his divorce was finalized.

David's previous wife, Shelly, was a highly intelligent researcher and college professor who, admittedly, did not care about how she dressed or presented herself to the world. She self-identified as more bookish, less fashionista. Shelly appreciated the help Charlotte so willingly gave in this area.

The girls flourished under Charlotte's guidance while shopping and preparing for parties, proms and the like. Charlotte would help them pick out dresses and styled their hair for them. Shelly even came into the salon and chatted with Charlotte as she worked on their hair. When out shopping with the girls, Shelly would encourage the girls to text pictures of outfits they weren't sure about to Charlotte to get her opinion. The girls loved their mother very much and chose to spend time with her whenever possible, but also loved being with Charlotte and their dad.

Charlotte realized early on in her marriage that it was best for her to be a really good friend to the girls and leave the parenting to David and Shelly. I interviewed the girls recently, who are grown now and have pleasant memories of their divorce experience. Because of the way the divorce was handled, the only concern they had was where to put all the presents they got from double birthdays and Christmases! Because the structure and boundaries were clear, the girls were able to thrive.

Getting to this place is easier if you are willing to do the work on yourself. Moving through the grieving process, learning your lessons from your role in the demise of your marriage and any dysfunction that existed will benefit not only you, but also your kids. Use them as your motivation to do the heavy lifting!

In order to achieve this blended family ideal, once you are through the grieving process, it's crucial to change how you interact with your former spouse. Many of my clients express frustration because they still feel they have the same relationship with their ex as they did when they were married. It only takes one person to change a relationship dynamic. Dr. John Gottman, a leader in the marriage counseling field, has decades of research around relationship dynamics and communication patterns. He developed his often cited 93.6% divorce prediction accuracy by setting up a "Love Lab" and watching newlyweds communicate (Prooyen, 2017). From this data, he identified four negative communication patterns that he refers to as the "Four Horsemen of the Apocalypse." These are 1) criticism, 2) contempt, 3) defensiveness, and 4) stonewalling. Of the four, contempt is the biggest indicator of divorce (Gottman, 2015).

In order to have effective communication, you first need to recognize when you are feeling emotionally flooded. When you are in a flooded state, the reptilian brain discussed in chapter 3 takes over and you are no longer operating from the logical part of your brain. This is when the Four Horsemen are likely to appear. Figure out what being emotionally flooded feels like for you and use it as your cue to end the conversation. Does your voice start to shake, do you breathe rapidly, is your heart beating faster, do you feel sick to your stomach, does it feel like your head is going to explode? Do you cry? Do you start to yell? These are only a few examples of what it feels like to be emotionally flooded. It is a very unique experience for every individual.

Once you walk away, it's important to calm yourself using some of the strategies outlined in chapter 3. You don't want to focus on the conflict but, instead, self-soothe by implementing more thoughts and activities that feel more calming. Once you have calmed down (it may take a day or 2), revisit the conflict topic with your former spouse. First you want to give him the opportunity to express his perspective. As he is speaking, there is a good chance you are going to feel triggered by what he says because, perhaps, it doesn't feel accurate from your perspective. Set that aside for right now. You don't have to agree with him, you just want to make sure you are clear and understand his perspective. It may be helpful to take notes while he is talking so you can stay focused on what is being said. Periodically, reflect back what he is saying in summary being careful to identify any unexpressed feelings he might not have included. For example "what I'm hearing you say is that when I didn't text to confirm when I was going to pick up our son it felt disrespectful and inconsiderate. Is that correct?" It's very important to monitor your tone and make sure there isn't any contempt in it. Contempt can show up as sarcasm, swearing, name calling, belittling, eye-rolling, and mocking among others. It is crucial that you make it safe for him to be honest with you even if you don't agree with him. This process is so important in communication and often missed in our eagerness to have our perspective heard. When conversation escalates to conflict it's because couples are trying to get to the solution too soon. You must take the time to hear each other out before trying to reach a solution. There is empathy in this approach that tends to be like water on the flames of anger. Changing your communication patterns that are ingrained from childhood is hard, but with commitment and persistence your efforts will pay off.

Once you have heard him out, you then want to share your perspective. If you can understand even one tiny part of his perspective, you should share that right up front. This requires being really honest with yourself and letting go of any agenda to be "right" or "win." For example: "now that I have heard you out, I can understand why my not informing you of my pick-up time would feel inconsiderate." In this response you are also taking some ownership. It is also important to use "I" and "we" statements when sharing your perspective as well as only speaking about your own experience, not telling him what he ought to think and feel or assuming you know his perspective.

I'm sure as you consider this method of communicating you can see why it's so important to be grounded and logical. I find that using the strategies Dr. John Gottman suggests for healthy communication are effective in all relationships, not just the relationship with your former spouse. Not only does this method reduce conflict, but it can completely transform all of your relationships.

Chapter 9

Creating a Life Worth Celebrating!

*L**etting go of the rear-view mirror, getting future-focused**

L When a client comes to me and is in the early stages of their separation/divorce, I find there are common themes. If the client was the one to choose the divorce, there is typically a lot of guilt combined with thoughts around wondering whether they did the right thing. If the client did not choose the divorce, or if they did choose it but it was sudden and from a place of trauma (physical/sexual/verbal abuse or infidelity/alcoholism/substance abuse), they will be hyper-focused on the "why." "Why did he cheat", "why won't he get help?", "why did I choose him?", "why is this happening to me?" During this phase, in every case, the client is spending most of their time looking in the rear-view mirror. My role at this stage is to sit with them in the emotion and help them to process what they are feeling. Using the exercise I described in Chapter 3, I gently help them bring their thoughts back to the present, get re-focused on what they can control. At some point, usually a year or so after the separation, they will start to shift their thinking and get more future-focused. This is my sign that they are near the "acceptance" phase of grief.

Deborah came to me a few weeks after her husband, Hugh, moved out. She had kicked him out due to the fact that he was smoking marijuana in front of the kids, was verbally abusive and depressed. He was also having an emotional affair with a woman at work. These were all relatively new behaviors for him and her hope was that he would get help and decide to come back. Well, that didn't happen. For the first year of our work together, I was focused on helping Deborah manage her thoughts. She was fixated on the idea that he would "see the light" and come back to her, despite the fact that he repeatedly told her that he had no interest in reconciling. She slowly started to accept that he wouldn't return, moved forward with the legal process, and eventually filed for divorce. As soon as the divorce was final, Deborah found out that Hugh was dating the woman he was involved in an emotional affair with during their marriage. She also found out through some friends that it wasn't an emotional affair after all, but a physical affair as well. Hugh had been dishonest about the extent of his relationship with his affair partner. He then took it upon himself to introduce his girlfriend to the children without Deborah's knowledge. Needless to say, this was a high conflict situation.

After some time had passed where Deborah was starting to take care of herself better, she slowly became more future focused. I started noticing a bounce in her step when she would come to therapy. She was smiling and laughing more. One day, much to my surprise and about 18-months after they separated, Deborah announced that she met Hugh for dinner. Deborah realized that she had no desire to bring up his girlfriend or any of the old stuff that had been rehashed ad nauseum during their separation. She said they just talked about co-parenting and issues with the children, and how they could iron out their co-parenting relationship. Deborah stated that she noticed as she sat there talking to him, she actually felt completely indifferent towards him. She stated she felt her life was better without him in it. She actually felt excited about finding new love! I was delighted for her! Since then, Deborah's sessions have been focused on rebuilding her career, getting healthy physically and "fixing her picker" so she can re-enter the dating pool when she feels ready. She is now future-focused.

When a client is in that early stage of grief, I typically will walk them through a visualization exercise that I will describe here:

Get really comfortable in a chair, couch or lying down. Close your eyes and take 3 deep breaths, in through the nose filling up your lungs, hold it for a second, then slowly out through the mouth and hold it for a second. Scan your body and notice if you have any tension, then intentionally relax that area of the body. Once you are feeling relaxed, in your mind imagine you are going up a long escalator. At the top of the escalator you see white, fluffy clouds that automatically part for you to walk through them. On the other side of the clouds lies your ideal life. Use all of your senses, what does it look like, feel like, smell like, sound like and taste like? How do you feel in this ideal life? Hopeful? Relieved? Excited? Really embrace those feelings of joy and gratitude. If you aren't able to get a clear image or a lot of details, that's okay. What you are feeling is more important. My hope for you is that you will feel inspired. When you come out of the visualization, journal the experience with as much detail as you are able to. It will come clearer into focus later.

Can't put the toothpaste back in the tube!

Cynthia came to me when she was thinking about getting divorced. She was in the early stages of her decision making process and had been having an emotional affair with someone she met while attending an out-of-town convention. She knew there was no future in this relationship, but she enjoyed talking and texting with him. He listened to her and seemed to care about what was going on in her life. He also made her feel beautiful and desirable. Alice hadn't felt this way in a very long time.

Through our work together, she was able to see how her affair was making her marriage more bearable and enabling her to allow certain toxic behaviors to remain unchanged. She was able to end the affair and she and her husband, Mike, got into marriage counseling while I worked with her individually on unwinding from her codependency and speaking her truth in a healthy and balanced way with her husband.

When I first meet with clients, I always check in on their self-care routine. Cynthia had a solid routine in place. Before coming to see me she had committed to a weight loss program and discovered a love of crossfit. She got into competing in crossfit challenges and always had a one on the calendar to work towards. She had a strong network of female friends who nurtured and supported her, giving her some balance. She practiced Transcendental Meditation on a regular basis. As we continued our work together, Cynthia got more comfortable saying "no" to commitments to which she had no interest in participating. Over the next year, Cynthia realized the more she was getting herself back, the less energy she had for the toxic dance in her marriage.

From the time Cynthia had her first child, Mike continued to live as if he was a bachelor. Friday nights after work started with happy hour with his friends in the neighborhood that meant he would come home drunk around 11:00 pm and fall into bed. Saturdays involved all day golf outings. Sundays he reserved for the family, but he was so tired and hungover from the other weekend activities he didn't have much to give. During the week he worked long hours. Cynthia essentially was a single mother living as a roommate with her husband.

I'd like to make a note here about affairs and how they usually happen. In a marriage, the emotional connection between a husband and a wife needs to be proactively nurtured and cared for to keep it healthy. Kind of like a plant that needs to be watered. When it's not watered, it dies. Another way to look at this is a death from a thousand paper cuts. The paper cuts are what lead to the affair and both people play a role in creating the paper cuts. They are the unresolved fights, the unspoken truths, lack of healthy communication skills, the fear of vulnerability, the sexual starvation, the emotional distance and missed opportunities to connect that exist in many marriages. When the emotional connection disintegrates and needs are no longer being met, in many cases, temptation eventually comes along with needs on a silver platter and the affair train leaves the station. Affairs are an unhealthy coping mechanism for a larger issue in the marriage.

While in couple's therapy, Cynthia could see Mike's efforts to change but by this time she realized she had grown out of love with him. She realized the changes he was making likely weren't sustainable.

Occasionally his new "mask" would slip and she would be reminded of who he was fundamentally. Mike wasn't a bad person, he just didn't seem to have it in him to really connect with her in a way she needed him to. Cynthia made an earnest effort to reconnect with him through dates and trips away to no avail. Cynthia realized she was staying in the marriage for her children's sake because she was worried about how a divorce would affect them. Once she was able to table this concern, she was able to analyze her relationship with her husband and get honest with herself.

When Cynthia and Mike were first dating, they enjoyed socializing with friends often and rarely spent one-on-one time together. There wasn't much dating in the traditional sense. Cynthia had evolved beyond connecting in this way and needed something deeper in her primary relationship. She realized she had outgrown Mike. She used an analogy that I feel describes this journey perfectly. Cynthia said to me in-session one day, "I feel like I am toothpaste that was squirted out of the tube and can't be put back in."

Cynthia was able to compassionately exit her marriage and maintains an amicable co-parenting relationship with Mike. Mike has realized he was phoning it in as a father and has stepped up his game with his kids. This couple actually has a better relationship as co-parents than they did living together. Since they are no longer involved in the toxic dance, they are better able to show up for their kids from a happier and more present place. Not only did Cynthia's kids sail through this transition with ease, but Cynthia was able to leave knowing she gave the marriage her best shot.

Accountability, Acceptance and Forgiveness

As I described in chapter 3, the final stage of the grieving process is "Acceptance". In my work with my clients, I always have this goal in mind because it represents a time when my clients are ready to step into the next chapter of their lives. This stage of grief does not happen quickly, there is a journey to get there but there is growth happening during that journey. There will be times when you will feel you have had a set-back. In the early stages of grief, there will be more bad days than good days. Later in the journey, you will be able to string together more good days than bad days. Eventually, you will have weeks or even months of good days and suddenly a wave of grief will hit you out of no-where. I reframe periods of grief such as these less as set-backs and more as layers of grief that need to be released.

I had this experience myself when I was at the end of my grieving process from a painful break-up from a boyfriend. About 18-months after the break-up happened, I was in a really good place and living a peaceful, joyful existence. I went to the grocery store to buy some bagged salad, and while standing there trying to find my favorite spring mix, my eyes fell upon the slaw kits. I could feel myself tearing up and barely made it to my car before bursting into tears. My ex-boyfriend made amazing slaw, a recipe from his mother. I am not a person who enjoys slaw that much but his was really good. That time the crying spell was very short-lived and by the time I got home, I was grounded again. When looking back on that experience, I consider that to be the last layer of grief. The grief from my ex-boyfriend is now part of my inner landscape and I recognize him as someone who helped me get to a place where I was ready to accept someone better suited for me into my life. The grief is not as prominent as it once was for me. I look at it through a healthier, more evolved lens now.

The concept of forgiveness can be a tough pill to swallow for many people, particularly in the case of infidelity, substance abuse/alcoholism or physical or emotional abuse. My clients amaze me on a daily basis with their resilience in surviving abuse. I completely understand why someone would refuse to forgive their former spouse after years of abuse, or in the event they find out their husband had been cheating on them without their knowledge. Studies show that this kind of pain is equivalent to the trauma of a war victim. Having said this, I find that reframing "forgiveness" as "acceptance" is sometimes more palatable. I also find in many cases, my clients hold on to shame for living in an abusive situation and allowing it to go on for a period of time, sometimes years. In these cases, working toward self-forgiveness sometimes means accepting "what was" and can't be changed.

Self-defeating thoughts around a past that you can't go back and change is one of the leading causes of depression and anxiety. There is nothing productive that comes out of beating yourself up with your thoughts. I find in the early stages of grief, this kind of thinking is more common and a sign that the trauma needs to be processed. I will sit with my client and gently encourage them to reign in their thinking to the "here and now" to areas that are more fact-based and within their control. After a while, this process becomes more natural for the client. I encourage them to be honest with themselves and journal the thoughts when they are spiraling and bring the entries in for processing with me in session. This is part of "unpacking" the trauma. In many cases, EMDR (Eye Movement Desensitization Reprocessing) is necessary. EMDR is a highly effective model of therapy used for trauma. For more information, visit the website https://www.emdr.com/what-is-emdr/.

Sometimes clients will get stuck in a certain phase of grief. This is more about resistance to accept what happened to them and can also be a sign that the trauma needs to be processed. Phyllis came to me after her husband, Ralph, of 30-years skipped town with a lifetime of her earnings and inheritance money. Phyllis was a high level executive at a software firm. In recent years, the emotional connection with her husband had been waning, but they had two kids together so she was hesitant to end the marriage. One day she received an email while on a work trip from Ralph essentially telling Phyllis he was done with their marriage and had moved out. He ended the marriage in three sentences without giving her the courtesy of doing it in person. There was no forwarding address. Shortly thereafter, Phyllis discovered that all of her accounts had been drained. We're talking millions of dollars. Ralph worked as a financial advisor and Phyllis had trusted him enough to give him signing authority over her accounts so he could manage them for her. He had also forged her signature to access accounts he didn't have signing authority for, an act of fraud and identity theft.

Phyllis hired a private investigator to find Ralph, who was living the high life in the Caribbean. She had him extradited back to the U.S. and started the legal process of divorce. Since the divorce was handled in family court, the judge ignored all the facts around what

Ralph had done to her (considered a criminal matter and handled in criminal court) and still required that she pay him half of her remaining assets and alimony! You can imagine the level of trauma Phyllis was experiencing. Phyllis stated that she wished she had left him in the Caribbean. At least she would still have all of her 401k!

When Phyllis came to me after all this had happened she stated that she felt stuck and unable to move forward. In my work with Phyllis, she was able to find the meaning in what happened to her and how she could use her experience to help other women. She also began to see how much her relationships were improving without the negative, toxic energy of her marriage. She realized how much her Ralph's energy was draining her and how much more energized she was without him in her life. Her friends and family started to disclose to her how much they had always disliked Ralph but were trying to accept having him around because they loved her so much. Her life was becoming more enriched than it had been in the 30-years of her marriage. Phyllis had more fulfillment and love in her life, which, she felt, was worth more than millions of dollars. She developed a yoga practice and eventually became a yoga instructor. She discovered a love of writing and published her first book. She started sleeping better and laughing more. Phyllis found more joy in the non-material than she ever had in her privileged life as a wealthy married woman. In this case, she was able to accept what happened to her and recognize she wasn't going to be able to change it. This was a long journey and took about 3-years for her to get there...but she was able to do it! She finally got unstuck by doing the work and changing how she viewed her situation.

My clients who hold on to the anger and resentment around the circumstances of their divorce tend to suffer more. Jill's husband Lenny left her for a co-worker with whom he had fallen in love. Lenny felt tremendous guilt and remorse over hurting Jill and their children. Jill admitted that they had a sexless marriage that had been suffering for several years and was able to identify in therapy the unhealthy cycle they both endured for most of their marriage. Lenny had a domineering personality and Jill rarely felt confident enough to use her voice. She remembered that she almost didn't marry him and had called off their engagement at one point. She also admitted to times where she fantasized about life on her own. In the 2-years since they separated, they had many conversations about the affair and her husband tried many times to make amends to her. Jill was determined to hold on to her anger, despite the fact that she had met and fell in love with someone who was much better suited for her.

Jill's children began acting out and showing all the signs of stress that typically happen when they are sensing their parent's distress. Her daughter started school refusing and would isolate herself in her room. Jill caught her cutting herself in the bathroom. Her son admitted to hiding his true feelings behind a false mask of acceptance when he was at home. Normally a calm, well-behaved child, he would get his aggression out by getting into fights at school. They both started refusing to go to their father's house. Jill admitted that she secretly enjoyed the fact that Steve was being "punished." I assured Jill that her children were the ones being punished in this scenario and would also suffer long term implications by carrying her burden.

It takes commitment and willingness to fully experience the grieving process and "lean in" to the trauma in order to reach acceptance. It's not an easy process but this is where the growth happens. The potential for a more fulfilling and enriching life is on the other side of this journey!

Learning to Enjoy Your Own Company

As you step into the big scary unknown of life after divorce, it can take a little while to get your "sea legs" as a single woman. It can feel scary and vulnerable to not know what the future holds. For some, it may be tempting to jump into the dating pool too soon before you're ready out of a fear of being alone.

When I was going through my own divorce, a friend of mine, Elizabeth, who was also going through a divorce at the same time coined the term "six-month thaw." Please note, there is no research around this theory, just an observation from my own experience observing friends go through divorce, from my own divorce, as well as what I have observed in my practice.

When you are nearing the end of their marriage, sometimes you unconsciously numb your feelings because they can feel overwhelming. There is a little bit of denial in this...putting your head in the sand in order to not face the big scary unknown that is your future. Shutting down your feelings can also help you cope with having to tell the kids, family, friends and co-workers that you are about to divorce. Once you are out on your own and on the other side of the transition, there is an emotional "thaw" that happens and those feelings can resurface with a vengeance. Your emotions that you have been stuffing haven't gone anywhere. They will begin to emerge. This phenomenon generally can happen around 6-months post separation but not always. The timing of it tends to be subjective.

The emotions that rise up during the 6-month thaw can be positive and negative and can feel overwhelming. Sadness, hopelessness, relief, excitement, fear, joy, loneliness and many other emotions can all be co-mingled. Clients tell me they cry more frequently. You may vacillate from one emotion to the next in a blink of an eye. What do you think the dominant theme here is? You guessed it....vulnerability. Am I starting to sound like a broken record? Many people will jump into the dating pool as a way of distracting themselves from these feelings. I call this "self-medicating by dating." The age of the dating app makes this unhealthy coping mechanism readily available. Once they feel the dopamine rush that comes from feeling romantic feelings again, it can be addicting. Oftentimes, one will pick a partner who is completely inappropriate for them at this time, or choose someone who is just like their ex but in a different package.

Karen married her high school sweetheart, Lou, when she accidentally got pregnant at 18-years old. Despite the circumstances of their nuptials, she felt she had an ideal, affectionate, loving marriage lasting for 30-years. She described her former spouse as "her person." Karen leaned on Lou for emotional support throughout her marriage and didn't feel she needed anyone else in her life but him and their kids. She depended on Lou to fulfill all her needs. Lou also provided for the family financially with Karen working part-time as a bookkeeper.

When Lou announced that he was unhappy and wanted a divorce days after their youngest child graduated from high school, Karen felt as if the rug had been pulled out from under her.

Shortly after Karen's husband moved out, she immediately jumped into the dating pool not only to soothe her damaged self-esteem but because she felt lonely. Karen had no sense of herself after Lou left her. Two years later she was in my office. She had been through a series of bad dating experiences, each one getting worse, until she found out that someone who she had been dating for a while and thought she shared a loving, exclusive relationship with was actually on Tinder and sleeping with three other women.

Not every 6-month thaw is as extreme as Karen's, but her story demonstrates how women are missing out on a wonderful opportunity to get to their identity back and fall back in love with themselves because of their fear of vulnerability. If you can lean into these negative feelings, which can feel anxiety-producing, I promise you, they will pass eventually. Just accept that you are going to feel the anxiety that comes from allowing yourself to sit with the negative feelings, but don't let the anxiety be in charge of your decisions! Taking the time to get to know yourself again and grow into the best version of yourself, while "fixing your picker" will enable you to show up in a healthier and more authentic way in your future relationship, should you choose to enter one. I suggest you start the process of meeting your own needs first.

As you are working on getting your identity back, I suggest you look at your life as a row of buckets. There should be a bucket for each of the following areas of your life (we will dig into this concept deeper later in the book in the "Values" section):

- Spirituality
- Mental/emotional health
- Physical wellbeing
- Relationships (non-romantic relationships like friendships and family members)
- Hobbies
- Work fulfillment

Your goal in the early stages of separation from your marriage should be to fill these buckets. Ideally you want them to be balanced out and relatively full before you entertain the idea of dating. It could take you a year or two to get there but you can make it a fun, enlightening journey. Wait, what was that I just heard? Fear and panic about being alone for a year or two? I ask you, what about your own company elicits such a response? When you are able to feel happy and content in your own company, that will shine through as you start to date. Having a strong sense of identity can completely change the energy around your dating life. You will not only feel more empowered, but you will be more discerning about who you choose to give your energy to.

Do you remember Karen, from earlier in this chapter? In our work together, she was able to craft a successful career for herself as a manager of an accounting department of a small company where she was able to financially provide for herself. She started taking classes to obtain her bachelors degree in accounting. She also built a solid friendship network with some women she resonated with, and bought a house on her own for the first time! In addition, she was able to repair her relationship with her children, which had become somewhat frayed during her 6-month thaw experience. She reconnected with her spirituality and found a church she enjoyed. She also realized the satisfaction of becoming a healthier model for how to manage life's difficulties for her children. This process was a much better remedy for her self-esteem than jumping into the dating scene too soon.

Reconnecting with Your Best-Self

I will describe what I call a "best-self" exercise that will help you get started with this process. Get out a piece of blank paper in landscape position. In the top left hand corner, write "Current Version of Me". In the middle of the page write "Bridge". On the right side of the page write "Best Version of Me".

Under the "Current Version of Me" column, describe yourself as you are now. Be brutally honest. List things such as "depressed", "hopeless", "tearful", "overweight", "scared". There might also be more positive descriptions such as "fulfilled in my work", "good relationship with my children", "excited about the future". Just make the list an accurate description of where you are right now in life. Try not to judge yourself.

Now, close your eyes and take three deep breaths. In your mind, remember a time when you were in the "zone". Life was flowing effortlessly, you exuded confidence and your self-esteem was at its healthiest. If you can't imagine a time like that in your life, imagine yourself there now. What does that feel like? Do you feel at peace? Joyful? Centered? Focused? Balanced? Grounded? What were/are the circumstances? Are you financially stable, thriving in your career, present and emotionally available with your children, family members or friends? Are you taking care of yourself physically? Exercising regularly? Nurturing your body with healthy food? Have a regular meditation practice? Are you connecting with your higher self on a regular basis? Do you have a consistent spiritual practice, such as prayer or attending church? Are you connecting with nature? Are you taking care of your mental health through journaling, attending a support group or therapy? Are you making healthy choices that honor your best self? Begin writing them down and as you are listing these things out, be very careful not to beat yourself up for not being there right now. You will get there again! Treat yourself with compassion. We all have highs and lows in life... it is part of the human experience. As a spiritual being living a human experience, the lows are where the lessons are so you'll come out of this as a better version of yourself. Once you get a full image of what that might look like, you are ready to build the bridge.

The bridge is a list of action-oriented items that are designed to move you from the left to the right. It is important to make these items tangible, clear, and specific. For example "exercise 3x per week" is kind of generic, "attend kick-boxing for an hour twice a week and walk once a week for 45 mins" is more tangible and specific. Some other examples might include:

- Wake up at 5:30 am every morning 7-days a week
- Meditate for 20 mins upon waking up
- Visit one church per week until I find one I like
- Attend one meet-up group per month

- Plan a trip to Paris for Spring of next year by the end of August
- Sit in the back yard with my back against a tree while being present with my surroundings for 30-mins every Saturday
- Plan an activity with at least one friend once a week.
- Write in my journal, including a gratitude list at the end of the entry, 4 times a week in the evening before bed
- Pull the guitar out of the closet and play it every Sunday between 10:00 and 12:00
- Walk a new nature trail the first Saturday of every month (download the All Trails app)

Once you are done, take a look at your list and tune into your body. Does it feel exciting to have a plan, or does it feel overwhelming? If you are feeling overwhelmed, set it aside for a while, we'll come back to it.

Now that you have all of the action items listed out, flip the page over and start listing your strengths. This is a crucial step because you will be pulling from your strengths to complete the action steps. Examples might be "used to hike on a regular basis and loved it." Or "I have a strong connection with my faith and spirituality." Or "I am an empathic, nurturing and caring individual." Or "I can be motivated and determined when I have a goal to work towards." This is part of remembering who you are. The beauty of this exercise is when you realize that you already are the best version of yourself. You just temporarily forgot her! So now you just want to get reintroduced. If you find this part of the exercise difficult (we are taught not to brag on ourselves), think about someone in your life who is your biggest fan. Ask that person to remind you of your strengths.

Now we are ready to address the overwhelm you might be feeling with this exercise. The final step in this exercise is to go back to the action list. Break it down to small, manageable bites. We want to set yourself up for a win here so don't bite off more than you can chew. Carve out some time on your calendar to start. Whether you choose to tackle one item or 3 items, you need to make a commitment to yourself to start. Write that part down on a separate piece of paper and tape it to your bathroom mirror or somewhere where you will see it on a regular basis. For example, let's say you decided to wake up every day at 5:30am. You decide to start doing that at the 1st of the next month. Put it on your calendar AND write it on a piece of paper taped to your mirror as if it has already occurred. "I wake up effortlessly every day energized and ready to meet the day at 5:30AM and have been doing so since 1/1/2020". This is called an "affirmation" and by writing it as if it has already occurred, you are asking for the universe to support you in this promise to yourself. Once you have that item mastered, you can move on to the next action item(s).

Rebecca was a client of mine who embraced this assignment like no other. Rebecca had been married for 6-years to Frank. She had been living under the impression that she and her husband were happy. On their way home from a weekend at the beach, Frank took the scenic way home to show her some sites from his childhood. The windows were rolled down as the soft summer breeze flowed through the car. Later than night, after they got home and had dinner, they cuddled up on the couch to watch a Netflix movie, after which he excused himself to go to the bathroom. Rebecca thought it was odd that he went upstairs to go to the bathroom. When he came back down, he had in his hands a pre-packed crate of his things. He handed her the key to the house and said "I'm leaving you for someone else. I am in love with another woman." As Rebecca stood there, stunned and shocked, Frank quickly made his exit.

Less than a week after this happened, Rebecca was sitting in my office. As you can imagine, her journey of recovery was very difficult. In the process of our work together, she came to realize that she had been living in denial about her marriage. Not only were the signs of infidelity clear, but she had been sacrificing many of her own needs to make her husband happy. As she got in touch with her codependent patterns, she saw where they were not only impacting her marriage but also other areas of her life. She got more comfortable using her voice and setting boundaries in the workplace and with friends and family. As she slowly started to climb out of the dark place, we did this exercise on a white board in my office.

Rebecca has always been a high achiever. She is a successful executive at her pharmaceutical company. Months after we did the exercise, she decided it was time to implement it. She came into my office with a "13-habits action plan." I reminded her that she was an over-achiever even with this assignment! I also suggested she go easy on herself if she wasn't able to achieve all 13 items on the list. She assured me she was going to commit to the 13-habits for at least 21 days (the amount of time for a change to become a habit). Low and behold, she was able to make habits of 12 items out of the 13! 18-months after she first stepped into my office, she had lost 100 lbs, had more balance and joy in her life, had healthier boundaries, was speaking her truth and was dating a new man! No one was more happy and excited for her than me! This is why I do this work! Rebecca is the ideal example of how on the other side of the depths of despair lies the greatest joy. I continue to be amazed and inspired by Rebecca's refusal to remain a victim of her circumstances. She did the work, figured out what her lessons were from her marriage and used them as a catalyst for change.

It is normal and common for there to be a period of feeling victimized from your divorce, especially if you didn't choose for it to happen. It is part of the grieving process. But it is not healthy to stay there. Eventually, you want to use your divorce and an opportunity to become empowered. This exercise is the first step to getting there.

I recommend you keep the pages you used for this exercise to reflect on as your heal from your divorce. It will be a reminder of how far you have come. It will also provide you with inspiration to keep making positive commitments to yourself to reconnect with your best self. Many of my clients keep a picture of the exercise on their phone to pull up when they are feeling down and need a boost.

Values Assessment and Redefining Priorities

Now we are going to break down the Best Self exercise even more by taking a look at your values and priorities. Do you feel you have an understanding of your values? Many people go through life without giving their values any consideration. They don't realize how their values are playing a role in their choices. Values often are rooted in childhood, either from what we were taught as children or from what was modeled for us.

Dr. John Gottman has stated from his research that they typically play a larger role in our life choices and opinions than we realize. In fact, even in conflict, oftentimes, there are underlying values playing a role, especially in perpetual conflict that can't seem to be resolved. Gottman states that 69% of perpetual conflict is not solvable (Fulwiler, 2012). Understanding the underlying difference in values can sometimes help people reach resolution to the conflict.

For example, let's say George and Susie have the same argument around their money. George is a saver and Susie is a spender. George was raised by parents who were older and grew up in the depression so they had a lot of fear around money. As a result, they lived a frugal life and saved as much as they could in order to make sure they could weather any economic downturn. They bought George a piggy bank at a very early age and taught him the value of saving any money that he was given. As soon as he had enough money saved, his father took him to the bank to open a checking account. His father showed George how to balance his checkbook and taught him about debt and how the interest on debt works. Because George's parents only used cash to buy things (except the mortgage on their home and their cars), they taught him that debt was a very bad thing. They put a high value on paying cash for things and living well within their means and passed this value on to George. When George got his first credit card shortly after graduating from college, he made sure he only used it for emergencies and paid it off quickly. He takes pride in the fact that he doesn't carry debt.

Susie, on the other hand, was raised in a wealthy family. Her family took pride in how their friends and society viewed them. They were willing to take on debt in order to have the latest luxury car or live in country club communities. They were comfortable with debt because Susie's father was an entrepreneur who had built and sold several businesses. Being viewed as successful and wealthy played a role in people wanting to invest in him. He needed to be able to live around and mingle with successful people. Early on in his career, he got a $2000 loan from his parents to start a technology business that he eventually sold for millions of dollars. Later in life he became a venture capitalist and bought and sold businesses for profit. He had an uncanny ability to spot trends and invest in the right industries at the right time. Susie's father was more comfortable taking risks and leveraging debt because of his entrepreneurial nature. He had weathered many economic downturns by taking on more debt and paying it off during the upswings. He never had any fear around carrying debt because he knew paying it off was just one windfall of cash away...and the windfalls always came.

Susie's mother often spared no expense with her own clothing, with household furnishings or when entertaining. She viewed herself as a partner in her husband's business by helping him build relationships with potential clients and investors, so she needed to look the part. Susie was also given the opportunity to buy whatever she wanted, whenever she wanted. She was given a credit card at a very early age and had no idea how it got paid off. She could use it anytime she wanted to buy something. She never had a bank account or understood debt. She inherited her parents' value around spending and wanting to be perceived as wealthy by others.

George often becomes frustrated by his wife's spending and lack of appreciation for debt and how it impacts their finances. Susie is aware that she doesn't live in the wealth she had as a child; however, with George, she doesn't understand why he gets so angry when it's time to pay the bills. Any spending she does now is strictly for the children so that they can have what their friends have in school, even if it means she goes without. That is how she learned how to show love. However, every month when it's time to pay the bills George and Susie have the same fight. If George and Susie could take a moment to understand the underlying difference in values driving this argument as well as the family of origin dynamics that created their position in the conflict, they might be able to reach a compromise.

I give you this example, because it's important for you to understand your own value system. This is part of understanding who you are as a person fundamentally as well as how you show up in your relationships. I'm going to walk you through an exercise to help you understand your own values. In the process, there may be some values that you may decide you would like to change. Perhaps some of the values that you were taught or were modeled for you no longer serve you. By understanding your values, you are better able to develop a value system that honors your highest and best self. In the case of George and Susie, there were positives and negatives that came from what was modeled for both of them. Neither were necessarily right or wrong in their values, but perhaps based on their current circumstances, what was modeled for them no longer serves them in their marriage. Perhaps George needs to let go of some of his fear around money and soften towards Susie, while recognizing that the marriage is more important than the size of their bank account. Susie would benefit from becoming more educated about debt and finances so she can become more of a partner to him in their finances. Having parents who get along, are joined and united as well as happy together is more important for children than having the latest iPhone so they can keep up with their peers.

Personal Values Exercise – How do I show up in my life?

(This exercise comes from the CDC Certified Divorce Coach® program, ©Divorce Coaching Inc., DCA-11, p 4). You can print a hard copy of this exercise here: http://eepurl.com/g6BBvT

The purpose of this exercise is for you to distinguish your personal values. When we are fearful and anxious, sometimes we make short-sighted decisions from this place. We sometimes look back on these choices with regret wishing we had made different choices. The more conscious we are of our values, the easier it is to make the right decisions day-to-day that are consistent with our values and better decisions for the long-term. Having a firm grasp of your values can also help you understand how and why you show up the way you do in relationships.

First, check off 15 from the list. If there is a value missing, write it in the lines at the end of the column.

		Family Happiness
		Health
		Competitiveness (winning, taking risks)
		Friendship (close relationship with others)
		Affection (love, caring, etc.)
		Wisdom (discovering and understanding knowledge)
		Cooperation (working well with others, teamwork)
		Fame (being well known or famous)
		Achievement (a sense of accomplishment)
		Wealth (getting rich, making money)
		Economic Security
		Financial Certainty
		Freedom (independence and autonomy)
		Integrity (honest, sincerity, standing for oneself)
		Inner harmony (being at peace)
		Creativity (being imaginative, innovative)
		Helpfulness (helping others, improving society)
		Personal Development (use of personal potential)
		Self Respect (sense of personal identity, pride)
		Recognition (status, recognition from others)

	Advancement (promotions)
	Spirituality (strong spiritual beliefs)
	Loyalty
	Adventure (new challenges)
	Gender Orientation (strong identify to gender)
	Involvement (belonging, being involved with others)
	Economic Security
	Pleasure (fun, laughs, leisurely lifestyle)
	Power (control, authority, influence over others)
	Responsibility (being accountable for results)
	Order (stability, conformity, tranquility)
	Sexual Identity (having strong identity to sexuality)
	Culture (race or ethnic identity)
	Efficiency
	Effectiveness
	Add:
	Add:
	Add:

Now, from the checked off list of 15, circle the 10 that resonate the most with you. From those 10, put an asterisk (*) by the top 5. Now, add a verb to each of those and write it in the lines below (ex: *Living my passion, seeking opportunities for fun, promoting community, supporting health and wellbeing, embracing abundance, practicing harmony, celebrating friendship, etc.*)

1. _____

2. _____

3. _____

4. _____

5. _____

As you are thinking about your values, you may recognize values that used to resonate with you that no longer do. You may also see how those values helped form where you are today in life. This is your opportunity to get clear on the person you want to be and how you want to show up in your relationships.

Once you get clear on your values, you can then write your own personal mission statement. For example, my personal mission statement is "I align with the highest version of myself by embracing change, creativity, spirituality and personal growth and inspire others to do the same." If you feel strong emotion while writing your mission statement, then you know you are on the right track. It should pack a powerful punch. It may take a few attempts to get it just right.

Once you have it written, put it on your vision board, on your bathroom mirror, on your computer at work, in your car, anywhere you will see it on a regular basis so that it reminds you of how you want to make choices and show up in the world. When we are in a dark place, we often make impulsive decisions from a place of anxiety that, while may soothe the anxiety in the short run, tend to be more short sighted and, in some cases, are self-destructive in the long term. Making choices that align with your values may increase anxiety in the short term but tend to be lasting and more enduring. Sometimes we need to be prepared to lean into the anxiety with our eyes firmly planted on the big picture that we want to create for ourselves.

Redefining your priorities

Now that you are clear on your values and personal mission statement, it's time to take a look at your priorities and how they line up with this vision of yourself. You may recall earlier in the book when I mentioned the buckets as they related to areas of your life. I discussed balancing the buckets as a way to stay balanced early on in your divorce journey. With this exercise we take it a little deeper, you will rank how much of a priority you typically assign to various areas of your life. You will notice that you likely assign a higher priority to certain areas than others. You may or may not have been conscious of how this might create imbalance in your life. That's okay, this provides a good starting point to see how balanced your priorities are for you. The more balanced the priorities, the more fulfillment and satisfaction you will have in life and the more likely you are to align with the highest version of yourself.

Following is a wheel showing typical priorities for someone who might be reading this book. If some of the priorities don't line up for you, feel free to change some of the headings until it feels more authentic to you. Now rank each of the sections from 0-10 based on how satisfied you are with that area of your life (this exercise comes from the CDC Certified Divorce Coach® program, ©Divorce Coaching Inc., DCA-11, p 5). You can print a hard copy of this exercise here: http://eepurl.com/g6BBvt.

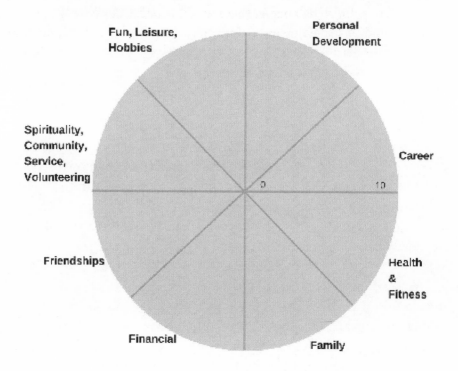

So how "bumpy" is the ride? Ask yourself the following questions:

1. Are there any surprises for you?
2. How do you feel about your life as you look at your Wheel?
3. How do you currently spend time in these areas?
4. How would you like to spend time in these areas?
5. Which of these elements would you most like to improve?
6. How could you make space for these changes?
7. Can you affect the necessary changes on your own?
8. What help and cooperation from others might you need?
9. What would make that a score of 10?

Striving for a "10" in all of these areas may feel like a tall order, but the idea is to achieve balance in these areas, whether they rank as a 5 or a 10. I recommend reassessing on an annual basis to see if you need to make any readjustments.

Chapter 10

Dating v2.0 & Managing the 6-Month Thaw

In many cases, when a client is thinking about getting a divorce, the irrational belief that they might spend the rest of their life alone might keep them stuck in an unhappy situation. I remember feeling this way at the ripe old age of 32 when I left my husband. I also remember having a strong intuitive sense that I would spend a long time being single. And I was right! But it wasn't the death sentence that I thought it would be then. I have lived a lot of life in the ensuing 20+ years! I have run a half marathon, bought and sold several houses on my own, traveled the world, was able to be a caretaker for both my parents at the end of their lives and make amends with them. I have fallen in love and had painful break-ups that helped me get clear on what I want to attract in a partnership. I went back to school to get my masters degree and changed careers. I built a successful business where I get to do purposeful work that is fulfilling. I discovered the spiritual beliefs that feel authentic to me and committed to a practice that keeps me on my spiritual path. Along the way I made many wonderful friendships that will last a lifetime. And in the process, I have learned to really enjoy my own company. I learned along the way that in order to attract my ideal lifemate, not only do I need to be comfortable in my own skin, but I must BE the person I want to attract.

All of the information and exercises shared up to this point in the book are to help you become that person too. I am sharing with you everything I learned in the last 20+ years through my own life experience as well as my training and experience as a therapist/coach. I can't stress this enough, it is incredibly important to be content with your own company when you enter your next relationship, should you choose to do so. I am a believer that not everyone is meant to be married and some people are just happier being single. The census data shared in the first chapter seems to back me on this belief. More and more people are choosing not to marry and to live happy single lives. Having said this, I also believe we are wired for attachment and most of my clients start dating again at some point, so let's take some time to "fix your picker" before you go back out there.

Most likely, the last time you dated was in your 20's and 30's. Back then, it seemed effortless. You most likely frequented night clubs and bars with your friends in your spare time where other singles were hanging out, thus, putting yourself in the path of many options for dating partners. Or perhaps you met dating partners through work, school or other activities. You probably based your dating criteria on looks, chemistry or what kind of car your guy was driving. In other words, you weren't very discerning about who you chose to date. Now that you are older and wiser, it's important to be a bit more cautious about who you choose to share your time with. Dating has changed over the years. Many of my clients and friends met their mates on dating apps. This opens up the dating pool quite a bit, but you also need to be very careful with your boundaries. I would like to take this opportunity to revisit the "6-month thaw" theory that I described earlier in the book.

As I mentioned previously, not only did I have a 6-month thaw, but I observed it with many friends and colleagues who have also gone through divorce prior to becoming a therapist. In fact, it was a driving force in my decision to become a therapist and work with divorced women. Since going into practice, I have noticed the phenomenon with some, but not all, of my clients. When you are in the midst of it, it can feel a little bit like a roller coaster. You may feel depressed or anxious.

You may lose or gain weight. You may lose focus and your sleep begins to suffer. You actually might sleep better than ever. Maybe you feel energized and are more active than you have been in years.

Many people will jump into the dating pool during this time as a way to self-medicate these emotions. The idea of being alone feels overwhelming. If you do this, you are missing out on a tremendous opportunity to get to know yourself and fix your picker. This is why even more second marriages end in divorce. 60%-67% in fact according to U.S. Divorce Rate Statistics. The rate goes up even more for third marriages: 70%-73%. It is normal to feel scared and lonely during a transition of this magnitude. You won't feel this way forever. Use this time to turn inward. There is growth happening and you don't want to miss it! The previous chapters give you plenty to work on in order to get you through it. I personally believe we need at least 2-years before we are ready to get involved in a serious relationship after a separation. Does this feel like a death sentence to you? If you feel that way about your own company, then who is going to want to spend time with you? Do the work...fall back in love with yourself... THEN date! In that order!

After you have gotten to the point of enjoying your own company, you will find that you approach dating with a totally new energy. You will feel more confident and self-aware. You will be entering a relationship more autonomously. From this place, you won't be so dependent on your partner to meet all of your needs. You will know how to meet your own needs with him there to compliment your already full life. When you are dating from this place, you will not only feel more empowered, but you will be more likely to enforce boundaries. But first, we need to figure out what your boundaries are going to be when it comes to dating.

It's important to be aware that people will present the best versions of themselves when dating initially. You want to try to see "behind the mask" before you emotionally attach to this person. Many of my clients who are dating talk about the "spark." They want to feel an immediate spark when they are dating someone new. This immediate spark can be misleading. This could actually be your insecure attachment system lighting up and giving you a warning sign that this is the same type of person who has caused you stress and heartache in the past. Feeling anxious and excited combined with feeling attraction can feel a lot like love. A slower spark is healthier. You want to feel calmer, more grounded and less anxious, while feeling some attraction. I have had so many clients who passed on the nice guy to date the guy they felt the instant spark with, then wondered why the guy was sending mixed messages or not following up on their commitments. These women are dating like they are 20 years old again! These guys are the avoidant types that will trigger an anxious attachment system. As a side note, my rule of thumb is to assume mixed messages are a "no".

As Maya Angelou famously said, "when someone shows you who they are, believe them the first time". Women will attach to the idealized version of the guy they feel the spark with too quickly, then spend way too much time and energy over-analyzing, questioning, wondering why the guy doesn't call when he said he would, follow-up on promises or disappear for periods of time. Or worse, ghost them all together! So you are probably wondering, how can I trust a guy who is showing me the best version of himself? Well, I'm going to give you the following 8 tools to keep in your toolbox to help you see behind the mask. Remember, there is an ocean of available men out there. You are only looking for one drop, but you're likely going to have to wade through a lot of water to find him.

Tool #1: Setting an intention

You have more control than you likely realize with intentionality. Not only does it help you get clear on what you want to attract in your life, but it helps you get aligned with what, or who, you want to attract. When doing this exercise with my clients, they often throw up obstacles based on past experience. These obstacles are usually due to fear of being hurt again. I suggest you let go of any experiences of the past and tune into the possibilities for your future. Imagine what it would be like if anything was possible!

Start making a list of all the qualities you would like in a partner. I suggest you focus more on how you would like to feel and less on the "package" he comes in. You might list that you'd like to feel loved, cherished, desired, or understood. When with this person perhaps you feel passion, laughter and intimacy beyond your wildest dreams. Perhaps you feel joyful, vibrant and healthy when you are with him. Be greedy with the list because you are placing your order with the universe! Once you are clear on how you want to feel with your ideal guy, you will recognize him when he shows up in your life, no matter what package he comes in.

Now, pay attention to how you feel when writing the list. What are some of the thoughts that are coming up for you? Are you feeling that it's not possible to attract someone like this? Do you feel resistance? Are you feeling that you aren't good enough or worthy of such love? Then you have a little work to do on yourself. You want to become the person this guy would be attracted to. This is a very important step in getting aligned with this person. The activities in this book are helping you get there. I suggest journaling these thoughts without judgement so you can look back later and see your progress.

Tool 2: When Should I have Sex?

The best answer to this question is "not right away". This is especially true for women who have been in long sexless marriages. There have been countless times that I have had a woman sitting in my office weeks out of her marriage telling me she has no interest in dating. Nope, none whatsoever. The idea of it makes her sick to her stomach. Then one hot and heavy make out session later the juices start flowing again and it's off to the races. It can sometimes happen just from watching a few romantic movies and remembering what it felt like to have romantic feelings. Once you become sexual with someone, the "getting to know you" phase stops and it becomes all about sex.

It's a good idea to decide upfront before you start dating how many dates you want to give it before you entertain the idea of sleeping with someone. While this decision is very personal to you, I like the number 10. I have found it takes about that long to figure out if what you are feeling is real. It also takes about this long to see behind the mask. Dating websites and apps are a great way to get outside of your circle of influence and meet men who may never otherwise cross your path. Many of my clients and friends have met really nice guys this way. Having said this, they are also filled with sex addicts. I say this not to scare you but to help you be aware. A sex addict or "player" is not going to have the patience to wait this long so you can weed those guys out by sticking to your boundaries.

Deciding what number of dates is right for you before you start dating is easier than waiting until you are feeling attracted to someone. You may decide to give it weeks or months versus number of dates. Whichever you choose, make a commitment to yourself when you are feeling stronger and BEFORE you meet the hot guy so that you will honor that commitment. I have found that most women get attached emotionally once they have sex with a man. It's just kind of how we are wired. There are women out there who are able to separate their emotions from sex, but they are the exception, not the rule. You are able to be more logical and discerning by waiting to have sex.

Tool #3: Pay attention to what he does versus what he says

Many of my clients have gone out with guys who have talked about how beautiful they are, how much they are enjoying the date, how one day they would like to get married again, they might even end the date with a peck on the lips and an "I'll call you later" only to ghost you later (ghosting is a relatively new word used to describe someone who stops making contact or responding to texts or phone calls). I'm not suggesting that these guys are being dishonest. They actually might be feeling that way in the moment. But you can find out how they really feel if they show up and follow-through on what they say they are going to do. A guy with a secure base will honor his commitments. He won't "over promise and under deliver." The good news is, if you are more anxious in your attachment style, being with someone who has a secure base makes you more secure. That's why you want to hold out for this guy!

Tool #4: Relationship history and ability to repair

The time will come in the relationship when you may discuss relationship histories with each other. Does he have a good relationship with his exes or are they all "crazy" or "psycho" (his description). How does he co-parent with his ex-wife if he has been married before and assuming they have kids together? Even if it was a high conflict divorce, is he effectively able to co-parent with her now? That's a sign that he is able to repair a relationship. The older we get, the more likely we are to make a mistake here or there in our relationship choices. But how we end relationships speaks volumes about how we show up in future relationships. If he speaks poorly about everyone he has ever been with, that's a red flag.

Tool #5: Can he "do" emotional connection and healthy intimacy?

While you are getting to know the guy, do you notice that the conversation seems to focus on him? Does he blame everyone else for negative events that have happened to him? Does he overreact in anger in times of stress? Does it seem like he's coming on really strong in the beginning, in an "over-the-top" kind of way? Does he profess his love too soon in the relationship? Does it seem like he's love bombing you? If so, it's time to hit the brakes. These are signs that you may have a narcissist on your hands.

Dating guys like this can feel intoxicating in the beginning, but they always wreak havoc on your self-esteem. Some of my clients have incredible difficulty recovering from relationships with narcissists. If you feel the guy you are dating may be one, do yourself a favor and research it further before you fully attach. Ramani Durvasula, PhD has done lots of research about being in a relationship with a narcissist. Her book "Should I Stay or Should I Go" is a good resource to help you determine if the guy you are dating is a narcissist. A nice guy can come on strong in the beginning as well, but the key difference with a narcissist is a) lack of empathy, b) over-the-top anger (rage), and c) lack of ownership or taking responsibility for his actions. A nice guy will also engage in a mutual give and take in conversation, which is a sign he has the capacity to do emotional connection and healthy intimacy.

Tool #6: What are his values and priorities?

Do you remember the values and priorities exercises we did earlier on in this book? While you are getting to know someone, it is a good idea to get a feel for his value system as well as what his priorities are and how they align with yours. Your values and priorities don't need to be exactly the same but they need to fit well. If you can get a sense that his wheel is relatively balanced, that means he has taken time to do the work on himself before he started dating. A green light!

Tool #7: What are your common interests?

Dr. John Gottman discusses a concept called "Shared Meaning" in his book "7-Habits for Making a Marriage Work." Do you have enough common interests that you enjoy spending time together? In the early stages of a relationship, there is a "honeymoon" stage. Sex and desire tend to be the focus. Once this fades, it's important to have a few things you enjoy doing together. For the things that you don't share in common, there should be acceptance and support for each other.

Naomi came to see me because she was considering ending her marriage with Gary because she didn't feel spiritually nurtured in the relationship. Naomi is a spiritual woman and committed to her Methodist faith. Before getting married to Gary, she enjoyed going to services on the weekends. In fact, she was initially attracted to Gary because he was also spiritual, something she hadn't experienced in her previous relationships.

When we were discussing Naomi's relationship history, she talked about a previous relationship she had with Kevin who identified as an atheist. Once Kevin understood how important Naomi's spiritual practice was for her, not only did he make sure she got up on time for services, but he drove her to church! Even though he didn't share her beliefs, he cared about her enough to want her to have this important need met. This was missing in her current marriage to Gary because, Naomi acknowledged, at the beginning of the relationship, she started going to Gary's Catholic church and never communicated how important her own faith was to her. I worked with Naomi to communicate this to Gary in a way that created acceptance rather than resistance. Once Naomi was able to communicate her needs more openly, their emotional connection flourished as Gary suggested alternating church services each Sunday. As you can see from this example, having common interests is important but you also must be willing to support each other and compromise when you don't have a shared interest.

Tool #8: How does he communicate when he doesn't agree with you?

The truth is, none of us like conflict. Unless you're dealing with a personality disordered person, most people recoil from conflict. Having said this, in healthy relationships, couple's are able to work through disagreements in a healthy way.

Is the guy you are dating able to identify and express how he is feeling or does he completely shut down when something is bothering him. When someone is more avoidant in their make-up they will oftentimes stonewall when they feel emotionally flooded. This can look like someone is checked out of the conversation, either by emotionally withdrawing, retreating or not responding to texts or phone calls. This can be a normal response if someone is feeling emotionally flooded and needs time to process their emotions before talking about them, but it can also be used as "punishment" or manipulation (aka passive aggression) by someone which is not normal or healthy. There is a fine line. If the stonewalling goes on for days on end and the issue isn't that serious and could be resolved with a conversation, it could be manipulation or extreme avoidance.

As you read through these tools, you may recognize in yourself some of these issues. Early in my practice I did couple's therapy, which was a wonderful way to understand how various couple's communicate. In this work, I found that sometimes couples who were married for decades still communicate like they did when they first got together in their 20's or 30's. Now is your opportunity to change how you communicate in your relationships with your significant others.

The following chart shows constructive vs. destructive communication patterns with specific examples of each. Do any of these destructive patterns resonate with you? If so, make note of the constructive counterpart and make an effort to change to healthier methods of communicating. (This exercise comes from the CDC Certified Divorce Coaching® program, ©Divorce Coaching Inc., DCF-3, p 7):

	Constructive	**Destructive**
Active	Perspective Taking Creating Solutions Expressing Emotions Reaching Out	Winning at all costs Displaying anger Demeaning others Retaliating
Passive	Reflective Thinking Delay Responding Adapting	Avoiding Yielding Hiding Emotions Self-criticizing

Hilary is a client of mine who was determined to fix her picker. She had the self-awareness to recognize her unhealthy relationship patterns and was motivated to work diligently to change them. As a younger woman dating in her 20's, she acknowledged that she tended to sleep with men too soon and regret it later.

As Hilary re-entered the dating pool, she used all of the tools listed above. Every single one of them! She was 38-years old coming out of a 15-year marriage. The last 3 years had been sexless. Hilary had all the normal sexual urges of a woman her age. She decided to try online dating, and hit it off with the third guy she dated, Jonathan. They had tremendous chemistry and all of her juices started flowing again, but she was strong and stuck to her boundaries. Jonathon started out presenting as the perfect guy, showing up and following through on his commitments. He was responsive to texts and seemed engaged and interested in her when they went out. By the 4th date, when Hillary hadn't had sex with him yet, he started to express frustration. Hillary was clear in her communication with him that she needed to get to know someone and be exclusive with them before having sex. Jonathan lost patience and started to become less reliable and responsive, eventually ghosting her. Hillary was grateful that she took the time to see who Jonathan really was. She is now dating Josh, a nice guy who was willing to wait until Hillary was ready to advance the relationship. She enjoys a happy, healthy, sexually and emotionally connected relationship with him!

Sex as a mature single woman and learning to meet your own needs

As you read through this, you may be wondering, "how can I stay strong while I'm waiting to see behind the mask?" We are sexual beings after all with normal sexual needs and desires. Especially if you are coming out of a sexless marriage, you may be eager to get back in touch with your sexuality since it likely has been dormant. If you never have really been in touch with your sexuality, now is a great opportunity to figure out what feels good to you so you can communicate it to your partner in the future.

As you are doing the exercises in this book and evolving into a higher version of yourself, I suggest you start by making some really good single friends, whether they be male or female. Having a tribe of friends that really get you and you get them who you can depend on to show up and follow through as you do for them can help you get through many lonely weekends. You will be more likely to attend meet-up groups, go on hikes, take classes, travel, etc if you have someone to go with you. When I was newly single, I figured this out pretty quickly and literally made it like a part-time job to find my tribe. It took a while but I was persistent, and now have a great group of friends who have been in my life for years. I am very grateful for every single one of them.

Once you have a tribe of friends to help keep you busy and fill your idle time, it's time to address your sexual needs. I suggest you start working on meeting your own sexual needs. Here is where I'd like to bring up the topic of masturbation. Let's start by trying this word on for a bit. How does it feel to you? Tune into your body and notice any physical sensations that arise when you sit with the word for a moment. Some of you probably have no problem with the idea of masturbation and may already be practicing it, but not all women feel this way. Does the idea of touching your body make you cringe? Many women feel shame about their bodies that is rooted in either a negative core belief from unhealthy body shaming, messaging from childhood or, worse, due to sexual trauma. This negative belief is inaccurate, but you may still feel it even if you don't believe it cognitively. Getting comfortable with your body by touching it is a huge step in your journey to healing and reconnecting with your best self.

I really like Regena "Mama Gena" Thomashauer's work http:// mamagenas.com/. I suggest you check out her work if you'd like to explore the concept of your sexuality in more depth. If you have severe sexual trauma in your history, I suggest you consult with a therapist specializing in trauma or women's sexual issues before moving forward with this chapter.

The first step in this journey is to get familiar with your anatomy. If you have extreme difficulty with being touched, sometimes it is helpful to start by getting regular massages just to get used to human touch in a safe environment. Once you are more comfortable, you can advance to the next level. I recommend you carve out some time to give yourself some affection. Perhaps once or twice a week for 20 minutes. I suggest you start by standing in front of a mirror naked. Notice your thoughts as you do this. Are you shaming yourself? Beating yourself up for putting on some weight? Noticing every flaw and imperfection? Just observe the thoughts as they flow through your head. Can you see how your thinking can inhabit you from fully expressing yourself as a sexual being?

Now, I suggest you attempt to shift the thinking. What do you love about your body? How does it function well for you? Touch your body as you have these more positive thoughts, lovingly caressing it. It may be more helpful to do this exercise without the mirror first, perhaps lying in bed, and work your way up to standing in front of the mirror.

Once you are more comfortable with your body, it's time to get more in touch with your genitals. I suggest you sit in bed with your legs spread and an overhead light on. Bring a hand mirror with you and take a good long look at your genitals to figure out where everything is. It's important to get really comfortable with your body and treat it with the love it deserves. It serves you well and brings you pleasure!

Next I suggest you advance to touching yourself more erotically. If it feels awkward at first, don't give up! Just keep honoring your time commitment to yourself to keep this exercise going until you get more comfortable. If you have never masturbated before, it might help to get some erotica to read or listen to in order to get the juices flowing.

Once you have gotten comfortable with touching yourself and bringing yourself to orgasm, you may consider advancing to sex toys. Vibrators are a fun, wonderful way to achieve orgasm. If you aren't comfortable going into a sex shop, there are many websites geared towards women that sell sex toys and will mail them to you in discreet packaging.

Chapter 11

Putting it All Together

The combination of having a great tribe of friends, developing hobbies and interests and taking care of your own sexual needs can go a long way in meeting your own needs. Some of my clients will also get a pet to cuddle with if they miss giving and receiving affection. Patricia is a 70-year old client who I adore. She is a child of the 60s, an artist and has a cool eclectic hippy bohemian vibe. She self-described as a highly sexual being. Her marriage was not a happy one, but the one thing they did have going for them is great sex. She was very concerned about going without it when her 40-year marriage ended. She said she wasn't really a "girlfriend" kind of girl and preferred the company of men.

Patricia attended one of my support groups and connected really well with the women there, much to her surprise. As she opened herself up to friendships with these women, she was able to see the unique emotional needs having a good group of nurturing girlfriends around her provided. With her art, her girlfriends, her vibrator collection and her newly adopted cat she has been happily single for years now. She has the occasional relationship with a man but says she is just fine living independently.

In closing, my hope is that this book and exercises provided will help shine some light on your path to recovery from your divorce. I also hope you are able to see how divorce can provide a catalyst for much needed and lasting change. In my practice, it is such an honor to watch my clients flourish after divorce. The clients who are able to focus on themselves and make changes in the way they show up in their lives tend to flourish the most. The clients who stay stuck in old negative patterns and who are determined to remain victims without owning their role in the divorce are the ones who suffer. This book was written for those clients as well. You CAN break out of that feeling of "stuckness" if you are willing to take some ownership and embrace change.

My hope for you is that, in the future, you will look back on this time in your life as a turning point of sorts and recognize how you reconnected with the best version of yourself. You will see from that vantage point that you had a "before divorce" life and an "after divorce" life. The next chapter will be amazing!

The End

Bibliography

Beattie, Melody (1986), *CoDependent No More: How to stop controlling others and start caring for yourself.* (First Edition), Hazelden Publishing

Brook, Tess (Cohesive Conversations), (2016, April 12), "Bill Eddy talks BIFF quick responses to High Conflict People". [Video File]. Retrieved from https://tinyurl.com/y4cnktpv

Brown, Brene (2011, January 3), "The Power of Vulnerability". [Video File]. Retrieved from YouTube https://tinyurl.com/ydyah3lv

Carnes, Patrick (2019). *The Betrayal Bond: breaking free of exploitive relationships.* (Revised Edition), Health Communications Inc.

Cooper, Pegotty & Randy (2017). *Reptilian Brain and Hot Buttons.* ©Divorce Coaching Inc. Certified Divorce Coach® Program, DCF 3, 3

Cooper, Pegotty & Randy (2017). *Redefining yourself- environment.* ©Divorce Coaching Inc. Certified Divorce Coach® Program, DCA 11, 4-5

David L, (2016) "Attachment Theory (Bowlby)," in *Learning Theories*. January 24, 2016. Retrieved from https://tinyurl.com/y6e5zveo (Online Source)

Duboc, Bruno (n.d.) "Plasicity in Neural Neworks". Retrieved from https://tinyurl.com/yxs93fru (Online Source)

Eddy, Bill (2014)- "BIFF: Quick Responses to High-Conflict People, Their Personal Attacks, Hostile Email and Social Media Meltdowns" (2nd Edition), Unhooked Books

Ellis, A., & Ellis, D. J. (2011). *Theories of psychotherapy. Rational emotive behavior therapy.* American Psychological Association.

Fulwiler, Michael (2012, July 2), "Managing Conflict: Solvable vs. Perpetual Problems." Published online at Gottman.com. Retrieved from https://tinyurl.com/y8xymvld (Online Source)

Gottman, John & Silver, Nan (2015), *Seven Principles for Making a Marriage Work: A practical guide from the country's foremost relationship expert*, (Revised ed. edition), Harmony

Johnson, Sue (2008). *Hold Me Tight: Seven conversations for a lifetime of love.* (First Edition), Little, Brown, Spark

Joseph, S., Mynard, H., & Mayall, M. (2000). Life-events and post-traumatic stress in a sample of English adolescents. Journal of Community & Applied Social Psychology, 10, 475-482.

Lake, Rebecca (2019) "How Long Do Average U.S. Marriages Last". Retrieved from https://tinyurl.com/y7vx942b (Online Source)

Lancer, Deborah (2018) "Symptoms of Codependency". Retrieved from https://tinyurl.com/yb6bufld (Online Source)

Livingston, Gretchen (2014) - "Four-in-Ten Couples are Saying 'I Do' Again". Washington, DC,: Pew Research Center, November.

Loder, Vanessa (2015)- "How to Rewire Your Brain for Happiness". Retrieved from https://tinyurl.com/y27n82cq (Online Source)

Mellody, Pia, Wells, Andrea Miller, & Miller, J. Keith (2003). *Facing Codependence: What it is, where it comes from, how it sabotages our lives.* (First Edition), Harper & Row

Prooyen, Eva Van (2017)- "This One Thing is the Biggest Indicator of Divorce." Retrieved from https://tinyurl.com/ya9l6n2x (Online Source)

Roster, Max (2019) - "Life Expectancy". Published online at OurWorldInData.org. Retrieved from: https://tinyurl.com/y8mw9oee (Online Source)

Seaver, Maggie (2019) - "The Average Cost of a Wedding is $33,391". Published online at TheKnot.com. Retrieved from https://tinyurl.com/y3mo7kpw (Online Source)

Shapiro, Francine (2001). *Eye movement desensitization and reprocessing (EMDR): Basic principles, protocols, and procedures.* Guilford Press.

Shiel Jr., William (n.d.). "Medical Definition of Neuroplasticity". Retrieved from: https://tinyurl.com/y3pk362m (Online Source)

Siegel, Dan (2017, August 9), "Dr. Dan Siegel's Hand Model of the Brain". [Video File]. Retrieved from https://tinyurl.com/y3drb7jx

U.S. Divorce Rate Statistics, Divorce by Statistics: It Doesn't Add Up. (2016, July 20). Retrieved from https://tinyurl.com/y6vjs426 (Online Source)

About the Author

Sherry Smith, LMFT, CDC® is a licensed marriage and family therapist, coach, author, speaker and podcaster in private practice in Charlotte, North Carolina. After a long and successful career in the financial services industry, Sherry felt compelled to switch careers and decided to become a therapist. Sherry soon discovered her true calling was to help women in all stages of the divorce process. Using her expertise in family therapy, her training as a divorce coach and her own life experience, Sherry has made the commitment to promote a non-adversarial divorce environment that is sensitive to the family system. She believes the children of divorce can become traumatized based on how the divorce is handled versus the divorce itself.

Sherry is an expert on helping women make grounded decisions while maintaining emotional regulation. She is well-versed at helping women facilitate healthy co-parenting relationships with their former spouses. She is also skilled at inspiring hope and purpose for these women as they begin to step into an unknown future.

In her spare time she can be found spending time in nature, hiking a mountain, trying out a new restaurant, listening to live music or spending time with friends and family.

To learn more about Sherry, visit www.divorceresiliency.com or check out her upcoming podcast "Stories of Divorce Resiliency" coming out in the Fall of 2020, available wherever you get your podcasts.

Made in the USA
Columbia, SC
08 May 2021

37562758R00064